Lifting the Veil

Lifting the Veil

by

Karen L. Cole

First Edition

A division of
www.HiddenBrookPress.com
writers@HiddenBrookPress.com

Copyright © 2010 Reflections on the Past
Copyright © 2010 Karen L. Cole

All rights for story revert to the author. All rights for book, layout and design remain with Hidden Brook Press. No part of this book may be reproduced except by a reviewer who may quote brief passages in a review. The use of any part of this publication reproduced, transmitted in any form or by any means, electronic, mechanical, photocopied, recorded or otherwise stored in a retrieval system without prior written consent of the publisher is an infringement of the copyright law.

Lifting the Veil
by Karen L. Cole

Editor – Richard M. Grove
Layout and Design – Richard M. Grove
Cover Design – Richard M. Grove
Front Cover Photograph – School photographer
Back Cover Photograph – John Cole

Printed and bound in USA

Typeset in Garamond

Library and Archives Canada Cataloguing in Publication

Cole, Karen L., 1943-
Lifting the veil / by Karen L. Cole.

ISBN 978-1-897475-48-5

1. Cole, Karen L., 1943-. 2. Ex-nuns--Canada--Biography. 3. Nuns--United States--Biography. 4. Teachers--Canada--Biography. I. Title.

BX4668.3.C64A3   2009   271'.9002   C2009-906142-2

In memory of my parents
Donald and Edith Traynor
and
for John

Table of Contents

Chapters:

– The Road Taken – *p. 1*

– Settling In – *p. 8*

– Classes Begin – *p. 16*

– Autumn Dreams – *p. 27*

– Painful Memories – *p. 35*

– Surprise Encounter – *p. 42*

– A Day In Bed with Bonnie – *p. 51*

– Christmas on the Farm – *p. 56*

– Bride of Christ – *p. 70*

– The Corner Turned – *p. 79*

– Challenged by Vanity – *p. 82*

– A True Calling – *p. 87*

– Of Losses and Gains – *p. 95*

– Staying Home for Christmas – *p. 100*

– Rebirth – *p. 110*

– Metamorphosis – *p. 117*

– A Plethora of Changes – *p. 122*

– Temptations – *p. 134*

– Budding Teacher – *p. 143*

– Final Vows – *p. 158*

– Meanwhile, Back on the Farm – *p. 162*

– And Back to St. Mary's – *p. 165*

– Another Fender Bender – *p. 170*

- A Better Job – *p. 174*
- Liberation – *p. 183*
- Summer with Judy in Red Rudy – *p. 196*
- The Torch is Passed – *p. 204*
- A Different Community – *p. 209*
- Tested – *p. 216*
- Summer of '69 – *p. 220*
- Stormy Weather – *p. 228*
- In Bed With Bonnie Again – *p. 241*
- Making It Official – *p. 244*
- Anti-War Demonstrations – *p. 251*
- Wrapping It Up – *p. 254*
- Wildfire – *p. 260*
- Going Home – *p. 264*
- Epilogue – *p. 267*

- Glossary – *p. 270*
- Acknowledgements – *p. 276*
- Biographical Sketch of Author – *p. 279*

Chapter I

The Road Taken

The hour-long drive to Eau Claire is a silent one, broken only by the drone of the car's engine and the rhythmical hum of tires on pavement. As we roll past recently harvested hayfields and bleached cornstalks, I glance at Mother out of the corner of my eye. She focuses on her driving. Her face is fixed, grim even; her hands grip the steering wheel. Behind her tired eyes flickers serious deliberation. Is she secretly relieved that I am entering the convent, leaving Barry behind with no real scene of anguished young love? I study her for a moment, regretting the quarrels that stained this last summer together. Does she regret them too? Is she concerned to give up her fourth child to a new life? Does she worry that I won't stay in the convent? Teresa and Terry are reluctantly along for the ride. At fourteen and ten they'll have to fill the gap of doing farm chores and household tasks I have been performing since Dad died two years ago.

For once I have nothing to say. I gaze out of the hot car, watching the familiar scenery zip by. Since I won't travel this road again till Christmas I try to imprint the view on my memory. I daydream of Barry, of our many drives along this route, headed to the drive-in or the beach. I reflect on his teasing humour, his tearful farewell – so many strong memories. I fight off a wave of self-pity at the great sacrifice I am making. My chest tightens. If only someone would offer me an easy way out.

St. Anselm's Priory is not far from home but contact with families will be limited for the first three years: few phone calls, one letter a week, one visit a month and two weeks at home during Christmas this first year. I fear loneliness more than anything.

How threatening the wrought iron fence surrounding the convent looks today, its rails topped by sharp fleur de lys. A girl could injure herself trying to climb over them. No doubt that's the point.

Situated in a quiet residential neighbourhood of Eau Claire, outlined by mature oaks and maples, St. Anselm's was formerly the home of a wealthy family. When the Benedictines moved to Wisconsin from St. Cloud, Minnesota in 1948, they bought it as their Motherhouse. The main building is a construction of brick and stucco with a large balcony atop the front porch, which is discreetly veiled by several spirea bushes. The side door is the one most easily reached by the semicircular driveway, the busiest entrance.

Once through the gate we turn left. Recently the sisters built Benet Hall on the large property, a simple wooden structure painted pale yellow. Mother pulls up close to the hall guided by the hand of a smiling young nun. Benet Hall is situated a couple of hundred feet down this driveway which is lined with reddening sumacs. A bed of mauve petunias and scarlet geraniums, made sturdy and lush by the recent heavy rains, edges the front of the building. Despite my mixed feelings about entering the convent, I can see the charm of this place.

Benet Hall will be my home for the next year. It turns out I will be the oldest postulant in religion. This simply means that my never-late-for-anything family has arrived earlier than the other families who are bringing their daughters to St. Anselm's today. We stand outside watching and visiting as the others arrive. Three more postulants turn up within the hour: Sherry from Eau Claire, Reenie and Paula, both from the southern part of Wisconsin. We four are postulants rather than aspirants only because we have already finished high school and will begin taking college courses tomorrow, right here in Benet Hall.

The Hall is composed of two stories – downstairs, a rectangular box which doubles as a recreation area and university classroom; the upstairs divided into a large dormitory and equally large bathroom with enough facilities to accommodate the aspirants and postulants. These are the young women like me who believe they have a vocation and have come to test the validity of that belief. The nuns at catechism taught us that *postulare* in Latin means "to ask." Aspiring – wishing for something. I don't believe I'm asking to join, more like following orders from God and His priests and nuns. I certainly don't wish for this at the moment.

The sisters living at the Motherhouse are not cloistered and they have gathered en masse outside to welcome us. They chat and laugh like ordinary human beings.

~ ~ ~

On a visit in the previous April we toured the Priory and were shown the public areas but only heard about the private ones. "The Priory is a warren of rooms on three floors. The sisters are housed according to their ranks," our guide, Sister Agnes had told us. "The novices, our youngest nuns, are on the top floor. They're best suited to climb all those stairs," she said waving a hand at the grand staircase. "The junior sisters sleep on an enclosed porch at the back of the second floor – heated in winter to deal with Wisconsin's famously frigid winters. Senior sisters have private rooms on the second floor, the largest one belonging to Reverend Mother Dorothy. So you see, as you move up the religious ladder, you move to a lower level in the Motherhouse. Going down is actually a promotion here." We chuckled at her touch of humour.

My older sister Maureen raised her eyebrows, surprised that a nun could make a joke.

We walked along the main floor hall, stopping at the library that faced the chapel, a wood-paneled room lined with shelves full of dark volumes, blue, green, grey, black. My reader's heart beat faster at the prospect of such an impressive selection of books. Would I ever have a chance to read them all? The sisters' dining room was adjacent to the chapel. From there French doors led to a smaller dining room used to serve the chaplain and special guests. A huge, old-fashioned kitchen with a couple of serving rooms attached covered nearly a third of the first floor. The whole house appeared to be beautifully furnished but sterile. It lacked the coziness of my own rundown home.

~ ~ ~

As the crowd shifts and mingles, I find myself standing next to Sister James Marie, my former catechism teacher. Her friendly face with its pale skin and gleaming grey eyes is encouraging. Seeing her reminds me of those days when my vocation was a mere spark.

For years I'd been thinking about doing something good for the world. At summer catechism classes when I was thirteen, angelic-faced Sister Suzanne inspired me. She was beautiful, with granny glasses framing her large brown eyes. Shaking a piece of chalk in one hand, and holding the other behind her back, she urged us to complete our tasks: "I hate quitters. When you're singing to glorify God, don't stop and chat to a friend. When you're memorizing the answer to the catechism question, don't start thinking of which position you want on the workup team at recess. Concentrate on the word of God." Beautiful but tough.

Her words made sense to me, as I sweltered with a couple dozen classmates in the old church now serving as the parish hall. The holders of the church purse strings deemed it a waste of money to install air conditioning in such a place, especially as there was a new church to pay for. All we could do on that hot June afternoon, when the temperature approached ninety, was to open the windows and hope that a heaven-sent breeze would bring us some relief.

Long ago Mother taught me "if it's worth doing, it's worth doing well." I always applied that maxim to my studies. Sister Suzanne noticed I showed a devotion to learning the catechism better than anyone. At recess one day, she called me aside.

"You know, Karen, I think you might have a vocation. You are the type of person who could truly dedicate herself to the service of God and His people." I breathed in her fresh scent, lilies of the valley.

I blushed. "Um, Sister, I have been thinking about it quite a lot. I do want to do something good for the world. But, Sister," I confided, "I really like boys, too. I don't know if I could be very happy without someone to love me."

She didn't miss a beat before answering, "Karen, religious people experience deeply the love of God which is richer and greater than the love of any man. Believe me, it is totally satisfying. Anyway, you must make your own decision but I can assure you that if you give all your love to God, He will return it a hundredfold." Her perfect skin glowed.

Old Sister Gertrude, standing nearby, her wrinkled face dissolving into a smile, added in her deep tones, "God is looking for young women like you to serve him. You must pray and listen for the answer. You may be one of the lucky ones to be called."

Lucky? Obligated is more like it. Yes, I felt a stirring when I was around the nuns, or when I knelt in the church, which was only slightly cooler than the hall. Yet I felt a different kind of stirring when boys were around. I'd watched my sisters, Rita and Maureen, with their boyfriends and I'd had a few of my own. I knew I didn't want to forego the joys of young love.

Kneeling there with the stifling air thick with incense, I bowed my curly brown hair, tied with a yellow kerchief matching my outfit. Even though I felt uneasy about it, I tried to push aside the thoughts. I feared God would punish me if I didn't heed His call, a fear fostered by the warnings of nuns and priests. Making out with boys? Making a commitment to God? Not an easy choice.

~ ~ ~

Sister James Marie rouses me from my reverie saying, "I'm so glad you're joining us, Karen. We haven't had a vocation from Spring Valley in a long time. Maybe all our catechism teaching is finally paying off."

I smile and ask, "Sister, where is Sister Suzanne? Is she living at the Priory? I've been anxious to see her again."

Her eyes cloud over as she confides with a little bow of the head, "Sister Suzanne went back to her home at the end of the school year. She is no longer a member of the community."

My throat and chest fill with hot acid. My role model left? The shock must register on my face. She has gone home? She has left the convent? She has quit? I thought she hated quitters. "The love of God is greater than the love of any man. Believe me, it is totally satisfying." Her words run through my head edged with my personal sarcasm. Okay, wait a minute, then maybe I don't have to stay either if. . .

I am about to voice some of this when Mother Dorothy, perhaps sensing some wavering on the part of this new postulant, says, "Now Karen, I think we should help you settle in."

This is my family's cue to leave.

"Wouldn't you rather be at home canning tomatoes, Mom? It's the last real break of the summer."

Mom hesitates. "If you're sure you don't mind. We did want to stop at the orchard to sample the cider and caramel apples."

I nod, nostalgia gripping my chest. I choke down a clutch of tears. Then I notice Teresa and Terry fidgeting, anxious to leave.

I finger the handle of my smaller suitcase. I could still escape but Mom would be so embarrassed if I tried to sneak into the car with her. I must be calm.

We all make an effort to act as if I am just an ordinary university student as we hug goodbye. If we feel the tears coming, we don't let them show. I bite hard on my lower lip as the new blue Ford drives away. I inhale deeply, eyes closed. Standing amid the crowd of nuns and postulants and aspirants, I feel utterly alone.

Chapter II

Settling In

A thought of Dad crosses my mind. Despite his flaws, he was a devout Catholic. He also had the gift of gab, a natural ability to chat with strangers; both of these I admired and developed myself. I'm not sure about what happens in the afterlife but I hope he's somehow aware of my big new step towards God.

And so, determined to make the best of the situation, I turn my attention to the other postulants, looking for a future friend.

"You're Sherry Carson, from Eau Claire, right?" I ask the girl with short brown hair and dark-rimmed glasses. She is a little shorter than I; her blue eyes are huge. She has a big family too which arrived only a few minutes after we did.

"Yes and this is my mom and dad, my older sister Prudence, my brothers Pat and George and my baby sister Joanie." Her little sister grimaces.

I shake hands with Sherry's parents. Her mother looks slim and youthful despite greying hair. Mr. Carson has a winning smile that spreads across his slim face; his snowy hair hints he's older than his athletic figure would suggest. He grabs both my hands in a firm, friendly grip.

Joanie speaks up: "I am not a baby; I'm nine-years-old. So there."

Doesn't that sound like home? I welcome this distraction because the moment of truth is here – I am well and truly entering the convent. Perhaps around the same time, Barry's family is taking him to the nearby university – only a short walk away. I tear my mind away from such thoughts.

I chat with the other new girls, especially the younger ones, who keep arriving as the afternoon wears on. I watch as little Yvonne, the youngest and tiniest of the aspirants, weeps bitterly as she says goodbye to her family. At least I avoided that, yet my empathy makes my throat dry and I fight for composure. These aspirants, ten in all, are still high school students of assorted ages, who will share Benet Hall with us. They will be transported to nearby Regis High School every day, a facility run by the Benedictine community.

Sister Agnes, the mistress of the postulants and aspirants, recognizes the familiar signs of internal struggle. "Now, girls, let's show you to the dormitory. You'll want to unpack." A junior nun named Sister Philomene helps me carry my trunk and bulging suitcases upstairs.

The dormitory has undergone a thorough cleaning before its new occupants arrived. The floor gleams, mirroring our reflections as we settle in. No stray dust-bunnies here; everything sparkles. Twelve beds with uniform green spreads are lined up six to a side facing each other. Sister Philomene whispers, "You'd better keep it looking this way or else," as she draws a threatening line across her throat. I search her face and realize it's a joke. The antiseptic smell of Spic-and-Span tickles my nostrils.

Sister Philomene, with cheeks like a chipmunk and a lopsided grin, leads me to the second bed north of a private bedroom. Again she whispers, "You're right next to the authorities, so you'll have to behave. This is Sister Freda's room; she's Sister Agnes' assistant." I'm starting to worry a little about how much truth there is in her teasing. She helps me settle into my little "cell," a bed, a small bureau and starched white curtains that can be pulled around the bed for privacy at night; she demonstrates. During the day, they are neatly pleated and tied back so the room is open and bright. I am lucky enough to have a window in my little alcove; it looks out onto the back acreage of the Motherhouse property. Some of the many trees are loaded with apples. Rose bushes with late summer blooms bring an unexpected smile to my face: it is lovely here.

I turn my attention back to unpacking. Despite the fact that I can't wear much of my old wardrobe, certainly not my jeans or shorts, I unpack piles of newly name-tagged underwear, including undershirts, which I've never worn before, two pairs of pajamas, a quilted green robe for modesty. Three bright aprons made by Mom, nicely trimmed with rick-rack, a few everyday dresses, skirts and blouses that I can wear doing chores or going for long walks complete my outer wear. Some of these are meant to ensure that my one black and white uniform won't get soiled. Naturally I will have to wash it at least once a week. Hopefully clean undershirts will keep it fresh. They go with the underwear into the second drawer. I also have a few pairs of sensible but good-looking shoes: new black penny loafers – fashionable but not flashy – and some tennis shoes for sports and walks. A thick black sweater will keep me snug in the winter months; a lighter one will keep away the spring and fall chills. All of us share a couple of wide, deep closets for our larger items.

Slightly raised voices draw my attention to two of the older aspirants across the room – seniors in high school. Bonnie, very fair with light brown hair and about my size, is helping Megan move in: "Now, Megan, you have to put all your personal items in this chest of drawers."

"That's it? Just the one? I have one bigger than that at home just for my underwear." Megan's voice is full of disbelief with a trickle of laughter running underneath.

"Well, we're meant to live simply here, you know. So put your toiletries, your mirror and a book or two in the top drawer, underwear in the second drawer, socks in the third and the rest of your everyday clothes and aprons in the bottom two drawers."

Megan, chubby, boyish-looking with auburn locks and freckles, eyes her with a furrowed brow. "Does it really matter which drawer I put them in? I mean, is this a hard and fast rule?" Megan's question immediately endears her to me. What difference does it make? These rules seem petty.

Bonnie laughs a little. "Well, no, I guess it really doesn't matter, so hey, do what you feel like," she says waving and beaming.

I can tell that Bonnie is also someone I want to get to know. Maybe these others girls are like me, with worldly desires still intact, full of confusion about serving God as they believe they have been called to do.

Sister Agnes, our tour guide last spring, who has been overseeing these activities, now calls us together in the big room downstairs, presumably to calm our fears and outline the rules. She tells us to help ourselves to glasses of ice-cold lemonade and cookies sitting on a large table.

Sister Agnes is slim and about my height. Fluttering her hands and moving lightly, she almost dances when she talks. A former elementary teacher, she is clearly well-practised at reading the riot act to her new charges. "Girls, we hope you will soon feel at home here." Her voice is gentle and melodic. "However, you have come to serve God, so we all need to work together to make sure you can focus on Him. Therefore, silence is to be observed upstairs at all times except for vital whispering such as 'Can I borrow a tampon?' You're human, after all. Silence is observed both in the Big House and here after Matins, the last communal prayer of the evening for us. Silence is kept in the Big House most of the time, unless you are given permission to speak."

I swallow a giggle. Does she know what Big House means in the outside world? Maybe my earlier impression of the fence was accurate. After all, they do call our little alcoves cells.

"You are not allowed to talk to the rest of the sisters unless given special permission. Since the postulants will be taking classes with some of the young sisters and even the novices for a couple of courses, you will be able to talk to them in the context of the classes and even to study together if necessary."

That sounds like a lot of silence for a big talker like me. Are we locked in at night too?

As if she reads my mind, Sister Agnes says, "We have lovely large grounds, as you can see. There will be volleyball, softball and eventually skating on the property. Most days we'll take you for a walk off the grounds. However, you will not leave the grounds alone ever or without permission from me or Sister Freda."

Right, so it is a prison then?

"All of your mail will be given to me to open. If it is acceptable for you to read, I shall give it to you. If it contains something which might endanger your vocation, I shall discuss it with you before handing it over."

Censorship too. I mentally groan. Ah well, Barry's not going to be writing anyway. I'm trying to keep a positive outlook, although there seem to be a lot of rules to obey. And Sister Suzanne is gone. Once again I experience a twinge of betrayal.

Beginning classes tomorrow will help. I love to study and the nuns have chosen a rich variety of subjects for us. I hope my courses will be my salvation and the needed distraction from the pain of leaving my family and Barry behind.

After our little pep talk, we head back upstairs to finish moving in. Silence reigns. It feels heavy, loaded with stories longing to escape. I look around at my new bedroom to be shared with almost a dozen others. Even in my large family, we'd only had to share with one other sibling.

A massive bathroom is down the hall with three toilets, five sinks and five showers. That's pretty good; much better than at home. It's right next to Sister Agnes' room, so I guess there will be no larking about in the bathroom either. Our whispering conversation will be limited to vital matters.

Sister Freda follows us into the dorm to demonstrate how to properly make a bed. Funny, I thought I knew this already. She is short with large twinkling grey eyes framed by wire-rimmed glasses that she often adjusts. Her round face and plump figure make her look like a well-worn Teddy bear. "Girls, watch this please. I'm going to show you how to get your sheets nice and tight." She puts a neatly ironed fitted sheet on little Yvonne's bed and carefully smoothes every inch of it. Is everyone else wishing, as I do, that it were her bed being used as a model? "Now the top sheet. See, my little ones, pull it up far enough so that you can do a perfect fold over the blanket, then tuck in the bottom. Now watch, here's how to make a French corner." She demonstrates. "Try the other side, Yvonne." Yvonne's hands tremble as she tries to follow her example. "Good. You'll find it's easy to have a perfectly made bed if you follow these instructions. You should be able to bounce a dime off your sheets." She flicks her thumb and forefinger on the sheet and nods with approval.

I look at Sherry and match her wry grin. Should we try bouncing dimes on our beds? I don't think such frivolity would go over well and since we can't talk up here, there's no point in trying to entertain each other. Sister Freda finishes Yvonne's bed and then, under her hawk-like gaze, the rest of us go off to try to emulate her style. She is such a paradox. She gives us each a little hug if we get it right but her firm manner indicates she will enforce the rules. Poor Megan had to try three times to get her bottom sheet tight enough to win her hug. Sister Freda announces, "The road to perfection, which we are on, is lined with ruts and mud holes and I intend to lead you to smooth ground as often as possible."

When the beds are made, we go to chapel, in our civvies for the last time for a while, where we join the sisters in praying Vespers and Compline, two hours of the Divine Office. Fortunately, they are in English, not Latin, as they used to be not many years ago. "Oh, God, come to my assistance," the head cantor intones and we all answer, "Oh, Lord, make haste to help me." Boy, that's the truth.

A tasty dinner of scalloped potatoes, pork chops, coleslaw and applesauce follows. A mood of uneasiness hangs over the large room, since although we may talk, we're a little shy. We make awkward attempts at conversation, mostly trying to learn more about where our colleagues are from and how many family members they have. The meal ends with a fabulous dessert that Sister Agnes calls plum duff. It is served with a yummy cream sauce, probably butter, icing sugar and other goodies. I'm amazed that the food is so flavourful. I didn't exactly expect just bread and water but imagined our diet would be simple and stark.

Once we have finished settling in completely and have organized our notebooks and pens for tomorrow's classes, it is 9:30 – time for lights out. I snuggle into my bed in the barren dorm, certain that I won't get any sleep at all. The clean sheets smell of being dried outdoors, just like home. Then ironed? I hope that's not our chore. I wonder what the other girls are thinking. I long to chat with them. Bedtime is so natural for that, the darkness providing anonymity. However, everyone is attempting to follow the stated precepts, at least for now, so the absence of noise paradoxically reverberates throughout the room. My weary eyes soon close – it has been a day of so many new discoveries, after all – and except for a nocturnal visit to the toilet, I sleep peacefully. I'm surprised when the 5:30 alarm shatters the darkness and the silence.

Chapter III

Classes Begin

We bound out of bed with the first shrill cry of the alarm – that is, most of us do – not Megan, who lazily turns over for a little nap, knowing that not everyone can shower at the same time anyway. And not Bonnie. She stretches each limb indulgently and finally emerges from her little cocoon, padding slowly down the hall, just as Sherry and I, early birds and overachievers, exit the steamy showers.

We dress quickly in our new underclothing and the uniforms issued to us by the community: for the postulants, black dresses with white collar and white plastic cuffs that we put on last. Sister Freda lauded their benefits yesterday: "They give the outfit a little dressier look. Of course, when you're washing dishes, you'll have to take them off and roll up your sleeves."

I lift my wrists and decide, okay, maybe they do. A little black bow tie completes the outfit. The dress is light rayon and not perfectly opaque, so a new black slip is essential; it goes on over the undershirt. Not bad, I think, standing back and checking my little mirror. I long for my large old vanity looking glass as I'm fidgeting around trying to get a good look. I guess the small glass is something else designed to keep us from becoming vain. As I pleat my curtains and tie them back, I notice the aspirants who wear white blouses with navy blue jumpers. From tiny Yvonne, only fourteen, to the larger and louder older girls, Shirley and Ingrid, they are whispering noisily across their beds. Didn't take them long to break the rules, I think with superiority. Megan and Bonnie, a year younger than I am, are the oldest of this group. Even they are nearly ready now.

There is an early fall chill in the air as we make the silent, pre-dawn trek across to the Motherhouse. The moon is still out; the eastern sky is just beginning to glow with an amber hue. I should have worn a light sweater as I'm covered with goosebumps. We enter by our basement door and hastily grab our net veils from the hooks, neatly labeled with our names. We are to wear these over our hair for modesty in chapel. We adjust them on the crowns of our heads as we climb the main stairs leading to the chapel.

Since the consecrated host, Jesus' body and blood, is in the tabernacle, we genuflect before we walk through the French doors, the main entrance to the chapel. The doors are shrouded with soft, white gathered sheers. We have to walk right between the symmetrical prie-dieux, or kneelers, behind which the sisters now stand on either side of a wide aisle facing the altar. The nuns are all in their places, assigned by rank and religion. Mother Dorothy sits in a place of honour next to the sub-prioress, Sister Cecilia. The other office holders, secretary and treasurer, sit across the aisle from them in corresponding places of importance. The rest of the sisters sit in order of their arrival at the convent. It reminds me of the descriptions of ancient royal gatherings, as Macbeth said at the famous banquet scene, "You all know your ranks; accordingly, sit down." Sister Agnes said yesterday that when someone is absent, her place is left empty. Reminds me of my siblings yelling at home, "My place is saved!" when they left the living room. The juxtaposition of the ordinary, mundane practices and the unusual rituals strikes me as curious.

Sister Myra, the novice mistress, sits with the novices on one side of the altar in more rows of prie-dieux, and Sister Agnes and Sister Freda across from them with their new young charges. The sisters are already praying the early morning office hours of Lauds, Prime and Terce. A series of psalms and prayers and sometimes songs form the basis of these hours. Like their founder St. Benedict, the sisters pray the entire Divine Office daily, even though they don't pray through the night as the early monks would have. The requirements of carrying on a busy life in the world – mostly teaching or nursing, rather than being strictly contemplative like the early followers of Benedict – has led to some adaptations. Lauds and Prime start the day, which would have been one in the morning. Terce should have been sung at three – we think six is early enough. None (Sister Agnes said it rhymes with "gone" not "fun") is sung at noon, as it is meant to be. It is the prelude to lunch. Vespers and Compline are chanted in the late afternoon, preceding dinner and Matins is sung at seven in the evening, instead of at midnight. Thank goodness.

By now even Megan and Bonnie have reached their seats and are looking suitably innocent and pious. One of the novices lights the tall candles and the natural smell of beeswax, a reminder of the Church since ancient times, fills the small room. It is time for Mass which will be celebrated by our resident Benedictine chaplain, Father Bartholemew, a wizened old gentleman with a natural tonsure. No way will he be a distraction for people like me who miss the presence of men already.

I settle down with my own thoughts and pray for guidance and strength to get through these early days. God, this is a foreign world, though so far a friendly one. Maybe I can handle it for a while at least with your help. I wonder what

Barry's first night was like. He's probably still in bed. I wonder if he's thinking of me. I like to imagine him lying there. Wait a minute. I'm in chapel. I'm supposed to be thinking of God, not man. I try to appear as pious as the others as I kneel with straight back and focus totally on the holy rituals. What goes through my mind probably does not show on my face. But, God, You know, don't You, no matter what the rest can see.

After Mass, Father leaves the chapel, followed by the cook and the weekly waiters and servers assigned to organize breakfast for the rest of us. When it is ready, a bell rings and the lovely walnut sliding doors dividing the chapel from the dining room are opened and the nuns enter. Following the grace led by Mother, they sit at the u-shaped tables with Mother at the apex, working outward according to rank symmetrically on either side of her.

We aren't there yet. Our breakfast is served in that same windowless room in the basement where we ate dinner last night. Some decorating attempts to make it cheerful – with bright yellow walls and inspirational pictures of Jesus and His Mother – are partly successful. It is near the laundry and as the aromas of cinnamon coffee cake and scrambled eggs waft down the stairs, they mingle with the fragrance of starched coifs and sun-dried sheets. The much-talked-about "odour of sanctity"?

In the interest of helping us to socialize and feel more at home, we do not have assigned seats and we may talk as we did last night, in carefully lowered tones so as not to disturb the sisters whose dining room is overhead and who are eating in silence. "Girls, girls, modulate your voices," Sister Agnes tells us as we grow too loud, a not infrequent occurrence as we get to know each other better. Two of us serve our group, picking up the food from the dumb waiter that runs between the kitchen and basement.

Today's eggs and coffee cake are only part of the generous

fare: fruit, cereal, both cold and steaming Cream o' Wheat or oatmeal. It will be difficult not to gain weight with such an ample diet, not at all like the sparse pickings I had imagined or read about. We are young, we will be studying; we need fuel for this work, or so Sister Freda reminds us firmly. If anyone appears to be watching her weight, Sister Freda speaks to her to see what is happening and to encourage her to eat a healthy diet while she is still "growing." I'm eighteen and really don't want to grow anymore. Fattening us up for the kill, I wonder cynically?

Even though we may talk, there is little time to do so. All of us have classes beginning at eight. The aspirants have to be ready to drive to Regis High School with Sister Clementine, a short, hefty woman in her mid-sixties. Besides being a teacher of math, she is also the community treasurer, a stern lady. She introduces herself saying, "You can check out as many books from the public library as you need but I'm not paying any overdue book fines. If you get your book back late, you can scrub the library floors." She sounds scary though a little smile plays at the corners of her mouth. When she says she is leaving at seven-thirty or they can walk – after all, it is only a brisk twenty-minute jaunt away – the aspirants are at the car, front and centre, book bags in tow, at the appointed time.

I watch them leave, longing to depart through those iron gates to freedom. However we postulants have our own university classes to prepare for. Last night we reorganized the room in Benet Hall into a classroom, instead of a recreation hall. We have permission to talk before and after classes, so without a chaperone to overhear, we begin to confide more in each other.

Though I've always been outgoing, I'm sure I'm the least pious of the new quartet. Clearly the others want to be in the convent; naturally they love God more than I do. At first I keep a shy distance, listening carefully as the others reveal a bit about themselves.

Sherry is the only one whose family is "normal"; that is, she has both parents still alive. Her older sister is at university in town and her younger brothers and one sister are still in school. She just graduated from Regis so being an Eau Claire resident, she knows a lot of the sisters already and knows her way around the city. Reenie, tall with long dark hair and glasses, comes from Austin, a town whose claim to fame is that a woman from the area believed she had seen an apparition of the Blessed Virgin and other people found her story convincing. There were constant pilgrimages to Reenie's hometown. She has only a father and a brother. Her mother died years ago, as did Paula's. In the latter's case, it resulted in very tomboyish behaviour and appearance. Though of large build, she is slim, loose-limbed and athletic.

Paula prances like a young colt around the classroom, eager to get started. Her short, naturally curly dark hair is slicked back in the ducktail style that some of the boys wore at school. Stopping to take a good look at her uniform, she announces, "We really do look like penguins, don't we? That's what we used to call the nuns at home."

Sherry warns her, "I'm not sure the nuns would like to hear you say that. I think it's a neat little uniform and quite comfortable."

"I don't think she was being critical," Reenie says in Paula's defense. "We do have to keep a sense of humour here, don't you think?"

"So, have you girls always wanted to be nuns?" I ask, cutting to the chase.

There is a din of responses to this which surprises me. Like me, they were conscious of a call to the religious life and believed that they had to give it a fair try. Does that mean they don't really want to be here either? My mind drifts to a day at home last winter.

~ ~ ~

On January, 1961, our newly inaugurated President Kennedy urged us, "Ask not what your country can do for you; ask what you can do for your country." Opportunities for young people to do just that were presented in the form of a Peace Corps. Volunteers would bring their skills to Third World countries to prove what a good friend America was to the world.

"I think I want to try that after I get my degree," my next older sister Maureen said one weekend when she was home from River Falls University. Her tightly-permed light brown head was bent over the newspaper. With post-secondary concerns filling our brains, life-altering decisions were our constant topic. I flipped through some brochures about St. Anselm's, the Benedictine convent I planned to enter in the fall after graduation.

"What? The convent? You want to come with me?" I joked.

"Hardly – don't be dumb. You know I don't believe in God. No, I'm talking about the Peace Corps that President Kennedy keeps mentioning. It's written up here in the paper," she said, turning the newspaper to me so I can see. Maureen's feet, encased in her white stockings under her wrinkled uniform, were up on a hassock. She spent a lot of time on those feet working in the nursing home, part-time job as she studied elementary education at the university a half-hour drive away from home.

"I'd like to go somewhere – maybe Africa – to help out for a couple of years. After I've done a little teaching here, of course. I'd want to be comfortable in the profession first," Maureen continued.

Maureen, a middle child like me, seemed driven by similar stirrings in her soul. I shared her idealism, except that, unfortunately, I did believe in God and my gift to mankind needed to be a spiritual one. Besides Father Riley kept reminding me, "You know, Karen, God chooses special people to do His work. He might have chosen you. So you must embrace the religious life. If you don't, you will destroy your own life and the life of anyone that you will marry or even fall in love with. You will always be hungry to do something more." Unnerving thought.

~ ~ ~

The young sisters enter the classroom. Except for a few who welcomed us yesterday, we have not met them. We are able to talk to them now, just as if we are co-eds on the outside. Funny how exciting that seems. I guess being denied the right to speak freely at any time makes the legitimate times much more valuable. As time goes on, I'm sure I'll break silence frequently but for now, I'm trying to make a good impression.

In the past, so we've been told, the young sisters were often sent to a mission to teach without a lot of formal training. However, since last year, Mother Dorothy decided to keep the junior sisters at the Motherhouse for further courses, not only in community and religion but also in secular studies.

Our own sisters are teaching these academic courses for the most part but the community is affiliated with a Catholic university in La Crosse in the southern part of the state, so we'll receive full accreditation. We're destined to become teachers or nurses, the two fields which are frequently associated with active religious orders.

Our first class is Hispanic American History taught by Sister Colleen. Her unhealthy pallor and guttural voice make me wonder if she has cancer or something deadly. Yet there is a keenness and energy in her manner that lights a spark of interest in her subject. She is a knowledgeable teacher and in this first lecture I gain many new insights. Even though the topic intrigues me her class seems an odd one. Why not a history of western culture or something? Later when Sister Colleen mentions that St. Anselm's plans to go to Chile to set up a mission, it begins to make sense. Chile? A chance to travel somewhere exotic. Maybe this won't be so bad.

The next class is music appreciation with doe-eyed Sister Laurel, who pinches her lips together like a coquette, then bombards us with the sounds of the classics we are supposed to learn to recognize. "Now, Sisters," she says, promoting the postulants a year ahead of schedule, "listen carefully to this." Playing a few bars on a record player, she gives us little mnemonics such as singing "Open-the-door" for the "Duh-duh da DUH" of Beethoven's *Fifth Symphony* so that we can identify and remember them.

Science is taught by good-natured Sister Verona who makes these mysteries fun. Father Bartholomew drones on in dry tones about church history. Although he is a pious old monk, he is clearly aging and has lost any enthusiasm for his subject. Only the fact that we are highly motivated to learn about Christianity's struggles keeps us awake and attentive.

Speech class meets on Friday with Sister Jeanette – fun for me, since it comes naturally. Those of us who wish can take piano or organ lessons from Sister Cecilia. She warns us against handing in work late or failing to do our best work but her joking manner and lovely features soften her message. I've studied the piano for two years and I am considered competent compared to Sherry and Reenie. Paula is an accomplished musician and is ready to begin organ lessons at once. Reenie, with large hands designed to make her a concert pianist, has no sense of pitch at all and often speaks of her musical abilities with self-deprecating humour.

One day as she begins to practise the scales, I turn to Sherry and whisper, "Wanna go over to the library to study?"

Sherry jumps up and grabs her books. "Great idea."

"I'm sorry, folks, I know I'm bad but I've got to practise," Reenie says as we make a quick exit, laughing with relief.

I love all the new things I am learning and I am amazed at times to see how they all fit together. My new colleagues are surprisingly appealing. Why did I think they would be bland and uninspiring? Between morning classes, we go to the kitchen for coffee or milk with leftover goodies and chat endlessly till we have to rush back to class. Sister Adele, our cook, a master of the art, encourages us to eat heartily. The promised games of volleyball and softball and challenging walks, long and brisk-paced, keep us fit. I thought monastic life would be much stricter.

~ ~ ~

On the last warm September Saturday, we don our most comfortable walking clothes – some form of cotton dress with comfy shoes – and walk the five miles to the site of the new priory which will be built in the country. The Benedictines believe their growing numbers need a place to spread out. The present Motherhouse is charming but cramped. An academy for girls is part of the planned complex too. After a picnic lunch and some exploration, we realize that we have to rush back on foot to be on time for Vespers and Compline.

With some swift steps we barely make it, especially as we aren't allowed to enter chapel wearing the casual, non-uniform clothes we have on. After a quick change, we race to our places. The rich smell of incense, usually appealing, makes me feel ill. Heat and exhaustion overwhelm me. Hardly have I collapsed into my chair, when I begin to break into a cold sweat. The bow tie at my neck is too tight. I struggle to hold my head up and suddenly, it falls into my lap. I have fainted – my first time. I wake to see Sister Freda bent over me, pushing my head between my knees to allow the blood to rush to my brain. After several minutes when I have the strength to raise it, she offers me a drink of water and swabs my face and neck with a cold cloth. The show goes on though: no stopping of solemn prayers to deal with a lightheaded postulant. However, all around me girls and nuns alike are focused on me while they mumble away at their prayers. It makes me the centre of attention and since I'm already getting a little tired of this absolute equality, I bask in it. At dinner, my fainting spell is the main topic of discussion.

"Didn't you eat enough lunch, little one?" Sister Freda asks.

"Yes, I had a sandwich, an apple and some brownies, plus a couple of glasses of lemonade. I think it was the fact that we rushed so much and it was so hot."

"Have you ever fainted before?" Sister Agnes wonders.

"No, never but I do remember feeling like that on Good Fridays when I was sweating in my winter coat and the church service seemed too long."

"We had hardly started Vespers, so it wasn't the length of the ritual," Paula puts in.

"Oh, no, I didn't mean that. I was just too hot, that's all." I blush not wanting to criticize the Divine Office and a little irritated with Paula for suggesting it.

"Well, eat up, now," Sister Freda, encourages me, "and drink lots of water. You were probably dehydrated."

A little attention was great, but now I just want to be left to finish my supper in peace.

Chapter IV

Autumn Dreams

Except for an occasional rain, the fall is crisp, cool and gorgeous. The maples are brilliant – scarlet and copper. Burnt sienna oak leaves cling to their branches long after the others have fallen. After classes we have to rake the lawns, no small task as the grounds are extensive. Dressed in everyday clothes with bright aprons, we are dazzling in the October sunshine. The acrid smell of burning leaves is in the air; our neighbours have been raking too. As we rake side by side, Sherry begins to reveal the story of her summer, a fleeting love affair with Dave Ryan, brother to one of the aspirants.

"Our family cottage is very near the Ryans' home by Lake Altoona. Dave is just my age and looks like the singer Ricky Nelson. He used to do odd jobs for my dad, who spent most of the week in the city while the rest of the family was relaxing at the cottage. We began to flirt with one another and the next thing you know, we were falling in love. At least we thought so," she confides.

How much our stories seemed to have in common – both of us deeply immersed in final flings. Her parents' reaction had been much like Mom's: "We don't care if you go to the convent or stay home and get involved with men. But you can't have it both ways!"

Dave had been the broken-hearted one, calling himself "Sherry's Clown" after the popular song about Kathy. He should have known better, since his sister Betty was one of our aspirants. Sherry, like me, felt she had to give the convent at least a fair try. I relish the chance to finally be able to talk to someone about Barry.

~ ~ ~

I'd been watching Barry Nelson for four years, waiting, wishing he'd ask me out. Now, just as graduation neared, he started to take notice of me. When we met in the halls in those last days of our senior year my heart seized. Since he'd shown little interest in me until now, I was torn between two urges: to embrace him or to clunk him over the head with my sociology book. "So can I give you a ride home after the baccalaureate services on Sunday night? Some of us were talking about going out for a drink at the bowling alley." Barry leaned towards me. I had to tilt my head to look at his towering six-foot-two frame. One sage-green eye was nearly winking. His football-hero build drew the attention of onlookers. I flushed with excitement as I gazed at his shy grin. He brushed a hand through his neat crew cut. Students rushing to class jostled us or glanced knowingly at this little encounter. They'd seen our relationship starting to blossom, even sooner than one of its principal characters did.

I glanced away to make the decision so he couldn't see the struggle in my eyes. The grungy walls wore that tired look of a school in late May, desperate for a good cleaning. The stench of sweaty phys-ed clothes buried at the bottom of lockers mingled with the stench of rotting fruit from unfinished lunches. Through an open window the scent of lilacs promised euphoria. As if under the influence of a narcotic, I struggled to pull myself back to the surface to give him an answer.

The bowling alley? Not a very romantic spot but in a small farm town like Spring Valley, there weren't a lot of choices. Later, we might stop at one of the favourite parking spots for young lovers. Shady Grove was just a safe mile away from Grandma's house. No chance of her looking out the window and reporting to Mother. It was a curved arc of a road with access to only two farms and it provided a private spot for teenagers to hang out and neck.

"Sure, that would be great," I gushed even though I was reluctant to start up a relationship so close to my impending departure for the convent. "But I'll talk to you about it later. Gotta get to English now. Collins doesn't tolerate lateness, as you know."

Barry nodded, touched my hand, and rushed off.

In my heart I knew we were already too late – not for class but for this new relationship. The urgings of priests and the encouragement of Sister Suzanne rang in my head, not to mention the fact that Dad would have been so proud of my entering the convent. Barry would be another Protestant boyfriend leading one of his four daughters astray. My intention to serve God meant a lot to Mom too, devout convert that she was. Father Hardy who taught her Catholic doctrine told her she was his most dedicated new member of the Church. So why had I even said yes to Barry?

~ ~ ~

Occasionally, when we are out for a walk, I look expectantly in the direction of the university, dreaming of a Barry sighting. It doesn't happen. I think of him often as I am falling asleep at night or, God forbid, when I am supposed to be meditating on spiritual matters in chapel. I can't make myself pray to forget him. I'm not ready for that yet.

Once I receive a letter from my former teacher and mentor, Ken Ames. His name is in the return address on the envelope and Sister Agnes calls me to her room to discuss it.

"Is this some old beau who is writing to you, Karen?" she asks, holding the unopened letter up. She cocks her head to the left and smiles.

"Oh, no," I say, smothering a grin, "he was my English teacher, a good friend of the family. He's a married man with children, nothing to worry about."

"I see. I didn't read the letter so I wasn't sure. You know, Karen, if you have old boyfriends, you need to forget them and concentrate on the love of God."

I swear this woman can read my mind yet I'm not about to confess what's been going through it.

"Well, Ken Ames is no threat to my vocation; he's probably just encouraging me to 'be happy in my work' as he always did."

"That's fine," Sister Agnes says, smiling as she hands me the letter. I look at her, grinning with gratitude. If she guesses anything, she is not going to harass me about it.

~ ~ ~

I grudgingly admit that except for the occasional stirring of sexual excitement as I think of Barry, I am content in my new way of life. When my family – Mom, Maureen, Teresa and Terry – comes to visit on the first Sunday of October, my younger sister Teresa, looking fabulous in a bright red dress, agrees. A touch of envy runs through me as I straighten my black dress and tie.

"I want to be a nun," she says. "It looks like a pretty good life – plenty of indoor toilets and showers, regular great food that you only have to help prepare. You aren't responsible for the whole meal. And there are no cows to milk."

"Yes, of course that's all nice but there are quite a few restrictions like keeping silence and censoring our mail." I look around to make sure that we can't be overheard by one of the nuns. They have served a wonderful picnic – they call it "a pickup" – lunch for all the visiting families. The food is spread out on tables and we go around "picking it up." We are under various shade trees on a perfect Indian summer day. Each family has a table or two as required. The five of us Traynors fit nicely around one. We have some privacy but can easily mingle with the other guests. That's the idea – one big happy family. In fact, as I look across the lawn, Sherry's father gives us a friendly little wave. I'll chat with him later. We hit it off on the first day.

Teresa goes on between bites of potato salad, "And you're getting your university education free, which is great because Mom and Maureen are having a struggle covering the cost of her schooling."

"I've got a job and a student loan, so I'm not too big a burden on you, am I, Mom?" puts in Maureen, nearly choking on her ham sandwich to interject this. "Besides, Teresa, for your information, Mother does have to pay a little each month this year for Karen's food at least. So the whole thing isn't free." She pauses and then in a more conciliatory tone, says, "But having had the tour, I admit it's a pretty nice setup."

"Oh? Glad you think so! Why don't you join us too?" asks Sister Scholastica, a junior sister who has just joined our group. "My sister and I are both members of St. Anselm's. It's wonderful to share the spiritual life with one of your siblings. My brother's a priest too in La Crosse."

"Oh, I don't think it's for me," Maureen brushes off her remarks. "I'm not as devout as Karen is. I want to do something – maybe join the Peace Corps after I finish my degree – but I don't feel any religious calling."

Sister Freda chimes in, her hands together, almost as if in prayer, "Sometimes it comes a little later in life and you obviously care about the welfare of the world. Maybe coming to visit Karen will open your heart to a vocation."

"We'll see," Maureen replies with tight lips, unimpressed with all this recruiting.

"And Barry?" Mother asks, lowering her voice, " You've put him behind you, have you?"

"Well, don't worry, Mother, I'm not sneaking out to meet him or anything, if that's what you mean. Sure, I think about him at times but for now, I'm concentrating on my classes and I'm sure he is too. I'm giving this a fair try, at least until Christmas. Then I'll make up my mind."

Mother's house has never been a place she could show off. Its outdoor toilet, worn furniture, cracked plaster and occasionally leaking roof will never make the cover of *Better Homes and Gardens*. She often said how wonderful it would be to have a child willing to dedicate her life to God. With a daughter in the convent she can really hold up her head in the community.

I know that I have to give the convent an honest try. There's a restlessness in me that won't let me simply "catch the nearest way" – go off to university, become a teacher, find a husband (or as giggling girls would say as we discussed our futures: "I'm going to college for a B.A. but I hope I get my Mrs. degree). At times I definitely want to follow that easier road. Yet I'm sure I can make an impact on the world. Is the convent the place for me to do it?

~ ~ ~

A few years ago, Dad gathered us together on Tuesday nights to watch Bishop Sheen on the new television. Through its magic the Bishop walked into our living room and spoke of how we could best serve God, the religious vocation.

"God chooses His special servants to dedicate their lives to Him totally. It is an honour that cannot be ignored. Young people who hear the call must heed it. The family offering a child to God will be singularly blessed with heavenly riches. Priests and religious are the backbone of the Church." The Bishop rubbed his hands as if in expectation of some immediate volunteers.

"Hear that?" Dad asked as the Bishop faded into a commercial for Tide – "Tide's In, Dirt's Out. T-I-D-E – TIDE!" "Which of you girls is going to bring these blessings to your family? Probably not you, Mrs. Logan," he said, nodding his thick auburn hair at Rita. Dad loved to call us by our boyfriend's last name as if we were already married. "You'll be married to Wayne before you're twenty, I'm sure."

"Oh, honestly," Rita responded, turning away with a grimace.

"Dad, I want to do that, I think. You know, maybe be a nun. I don't know for sure yet but I think about it," I said as if confessing a fault.

His glowing chubby face broke into a huge grin.

"Good, good, that's my girl, but you're going to have to give up the boys you know." He gave me a little one-armed hug; I could smell his last cigarette, an oddly appealing odour.

"I s'pose."

Being a middle child made me want to achieve something beyond my older siblings, something to make the world take notice. I'd been a top student in school; I'd been a success in forensics; I played my sax in the dance band, but being a nun, that would be unusual; the world would be impressed, wouldn't they? This niggling feeling about it kept me on edge throughout high school, a strange mixture of curiosity and fear.

~ ~ ~

"Mom, I keep telling you," I repeat, "I'm staying till Christmas at least and so far the convent isn't as bad I expected. Maybe I'll stay forever. Who knows?"

That satisfies her, for she breaks into a big smile and hugs me hard, something she doesn't do very often. When we part, I notice that the half-frown that characterized her face much of last summer is gone. It is smooth and serene. It can't be easy for her with Teresa and Terry still at home. She is working full-time as a clerk in a clothing store for subsistence wages yet she doesn't complain. She was not even forty-four when Dad died leaving her the mainstay of the family and now, I – the oldest of the young ones – am no longer around to help out. Obviously, it is taking its toll on Teresa and Maureen as well. I have an easy life, I can see and there is no way I dare to complain.

Chapter V

Painful Memories

Except for our welcome walks and Saturday science labs at Regis, the postulants don't get out much. Making the bed on Friday morning, I peek out my window past fall's florid sumacs to the world beyond the fence, the world I am missing out on. The mere thought of leaving the grounds brings a delicious sense of release, underlined by a little guilt about cheating on the deity I am trying to serve. I look forward to Sister Verona's class, Introduction to Science, a taste of all the sciences. Now we are concentrating on physics, which I had bypassed in high school so I could study German instead. I am learning all there is to know about levers, pulleys, belts and gears. How this will help me as a nun, I'm not sure, but my mom was the handy one around our house, so she must have known all this. I hope they don't make me teach it though.

Sherry often reminds us of her local upbringing. She rambles on with her high school stories, occupying the short drives. "Father Finnegan is a good friend of our family. He comes over to dinner about once a month, my aunt works in the office and Sister Simone was always my favourite teacher and . . ." On and on she natters. If nothing else I'll learn a lesson about patience and tolerance: "Love endures all things," as the scripture says.

Once Reenie makes a snide comment: "Well, we were all big wheels in our own high schools, Sherry, but none of that matters here. We're here to turn our backs on all that human glory. The only honours that matter now are those related to the spirit."

"Really, don't be so sarcastic, Reenie," Sherry says. "I was only telling you about some of the people I knew at Regis; besides I was talking to Karen."

"I'll bet it's hard to leave your schools behind," Sister Lily, a wren-like junior sister who is driving the station wagon, breaks in. "I came in my freshman year, so I spent my whole high school career at Regis too. Funny that we never had any classes together, Sherry." Sister Lily, as delicate as her name, strikes just the right conciliatory note in this little confrontation.

"No, though I do remember seeing you around. Didn't you take English from Sister Simone in senior year?" And Sherry is off again on Regis recollections while Reenie and I roll our eyes. Paula just closes hers, either meditating or trying to avoid the argument altogether. She and Sherry have already gone a few verbal rounds. Even though we share the goal of sanctity, we are human. Personality conflicts are all too common.

~ ~ ~

We postulants are studying literature as well as public speaking. Because of that we learn there will occasionally be some perks. Sister Agnes calls us together after classes one day in the living room of Benet Hall.

"Well, girls, I think it's time we enriched your culture a bit. The university is putting on *Our Town* by Thornton Wilder this week and we have tickets for you for Thursday night. How do you like that idea?"

I feel hot. Colour drains from my face. I am excited and terrified in equal measures. What if I run into Barry? I steal a glance at Sherry who is watching me, knowing what I am thinking. Since the others are showing their delight, I take a deep breath and say, "That's great! I didn't know that we'd get to do things like that." Barry aside, I've always loved the play.

"Oh," Sister Agnes responds with a sly smile, "you thought we were going to keep you locked up all the time!"

"No, no," I say, a bit embarrassed. " I didn't mean that. I just, uh. . ."

"It's okay, I understand," Sister Agnes nods. "Sister Freda will go with you."

Not surprisingly, they aren't going to send us out into the world without a chaperone but we aren't complaining; we are too excited. It will be wonderful to see some live theatre, even if we don't sight any old boyfriends.

That night as I toss in bed, memories of Barry ward off sleep. I retrace the romantic moments at the movies and in his car that we shared last summer.

~ ~ ~

Barry called me often in those magic months. No longer did I have to drive myself to the Friday night dances at Hersey, the nearby teenage hangout, hoping to be noticed by him, to dance with him, especially a slow one. We entered and left together and in every slow dance, I could barely breathe, held prisoner in his embrace as I stretched to place my head on his too-tall shoulder. I prayed my light summer dresses weren't rank with the odour of perspiration. Warmth and desire flooded me as we held hands while watching *Gone with the Wind* and I dreamt of playing Scarlett to his Rhett. Then an hour or so of parking in the driveway making up for all those years of longing.

"Yeah," he said, on one of these occasions, coming up for air. "I used to sit in sociology class and think of you." His right eye was half-closed again as if he couldn't quite face me. "I always wanted to ask you out."

"Why didn't you, for heaven's sake? Couldn't you tell I was aching to have you ask me?"

"Nope. I dunno. I guess I was shy and you were always flirting with other guys."

"Just trying to get your attention, I'm sure." I looked up at his soulful eyes, hooded by puffy lids and trimmed with lovely long lashes.

"And then," he said, looking down and tracing our initials on my arm with his finger, "well, you know. . . the convent thing."

This was rough terrain for us. Of course we both knew I planned to enter the convent in September and it was already late June but we tried to avoid the subject.

"Oh, well, yes. Let's not think about that right now. I want to do other things," I teased, pulling his long face towards me for a kiss. I buried my hands in his hair, inhaled his Old Spice and focused on the lover at hand.

~ ~ ~

Barry Nelson wasn't my first boyfriend; there were others. Bill Howe offered me his class ring more times than I care to recollect. Once, he slipped it on a stick of Doublemint gum and handed it to me between classes. At that time, I didn't want to go steady with anyone. I enjoyed dating – first the thrill of the chase, then roller-skating and dancing, necking in back seats.

Like most teenagers of the 60's, I couldn't wait to get home from school and flip on the TV to watch Dick Clark in American Bandstand. Before doing the household chores, my sisters sang along with the popular songs or listened to new ones that Dick picked as future winners. "Number one with a bullet!" We girls danced together.

On Saturday nights the whole family turned its attention to the Lawrence Welk Show. We four Traynor girls saw the Lennon Sisters as role models. Before Rita married Wayne and Maureen went off to university, we tried to harmonize as the Lennons did. We matched them in age and we dreamed that we might be discovered someday. Our family would be as rich as theirs. Our main practice time was over the dishes in the evening. None of us played the piano well so we performed *a capella*. We thought we were pretty good, but no one ever came knocking at the door with contract in hand.

~ ~ ~

Sunday evenings, we knelt on the threadbare carpet in the living room and prayed the rosary, taking turns leading the long prayers. Terry babbled away in that style that young boys have, when none of the prayers made any sense. Teresa half-sprawled on the couch as the endless droning went on. I straightened my back, kneeling upright, feeling so devout. I wanted to get closer to God somehow. It was almost like being alone with a boyfriend. Was Dad peeking at me during the rosary hoping that I would be the daughter to bring the family heavenly riches? He probably wished for a few earthly ones, too, as we all did. Farming was not lucrative in those days and he was not a prosperous real estate salesman.

Then suddenly in late March, 1959, Dad became very ill. He hardly left the couch all Easter Sunday. Monday morning, Mom tried to rouse him but decided to let him sleep, since he seemed so ill. After finishing chores alone, she realized he was unconscious – he had lapsed into a coma. Mom called an ambulance to rush him to the nearest hospital twenty miles away. At first we thought it was insulin shock but a spinal tap in the late afternoon revealed that he suffered from spinal meningitis, caused by an untreated ear infection. *An ear infection.* He'd suffered with it for more than a week, but didn't go to the doctor until the virus had spread. His diabetic body couldn't fight it alone.

That foggy night was the longest of my life. The mist hanging over nature clouded my heart and mind. I dared not think of the worst outcome. When we looked at Dad sleeping peacefully, he seemed normal, kicking the covers off his feet as he always did, a habit I shared with him. But treatment didn't rouse him. We hung around the hospital till the wee hours, praying for the best, till Mother sent us home for a few hours' sleep. Once there, I promised myself I was going to do something in my life to make Dad proud. The next morning he was rushed to the Mayo Clinic in Rochester, Minnesota. Despite two hours of the best medical care in the Midwest, he was gone.

So shocking, unexpected. Early that afternoon Dad's two sisters drove into the yard. We watched them walking solemnly to the door, anxious to hear their tidings, afraid to hear the worst.

Calmly Aunt Bonnie spoke: "Girls, your daddy is dead."

Confusion filled my mind. What did it mean? We clutched one another for support. Rita wept uncontrollably. I longed to cry but the tears that would have relieved the dull pain remained locked inside. My brain spiraled downward into a chasm of disbelief. Why did God do this to him, to us? Dad was only forty-seven years old. How could this be? Surely God would take care of us. But life would be so empty without Dad; I couldn't imagine it.

After the initial shock, we tried doing small tasks to turn our minds from the reality of death. Terry and Teresa had gone to school that day. Who would break the news to them?

Just before the youngest two returned home, Dad's brother arrived with Mom and Jim. Mother gathered all of us around her in a wide embrace. Instead of weeping, she was strength personified. "Children," she said, "this is God's will and we have to accept it." I marvelled, suddenly realizing that she, not Dad, was the true backbone of the family.

The traditional rites following a death – the wake, the Mass, the burial – helped confirm the reality of our loss. I seethed at the funeral home when I heard a schoolmate whisper to another, "Sad, but now maybe that family will have something." This honest but cruel comment released something in me. Finally, the dam broke and I sobbed audibly till someone led me into a private area with a fresh box of Kleenexes.

The next day I stood over Dad's grave weeping. The stingy April sun offered light without warmth, without the power to dry the thawing earth. The crowd of mourners was huge. They couldn't console me. I felt angry Dad hadn't taken the steps to avoid this outcome. I knew it would take years before I completely forgave him.

Chapter VI

Surprise Encounter

One scorching Friday afternoon in July, Teresa turned to me between sips of lemonade. "Are you going out with Barry again tonight?" She took another sip and patted her lips. "Because if you're not, I thought maybe you and I could go to Hersey together."

"Aren't you a little young for Hersey?" I asked, looking her over. Suddenly, she'd become a young woman with softly bulging breasts, slim waist and unlike her sisters, a flat tummy, since she always followed Dad's orders to "Stand up straight and think 'in'." At fourteen, Teresa was probably older than I had been at her age. Dad's death two years ago made us all grow up a little faster. Her blue eyes glittered out of her pale face with the sharply curved chin just touched by her light brown hair. I quietly noted that she was pretty.

"And yes, of course, I'm going out with him tonight. It's Friday night, after all."

"Okay, I just wondered. I thought this was just a little fling. You're still going to the convent in September though, right?" She pursed her lips.

I hated that question. Yes, sure but for a couple of months, I wanted to savour being involved with Barry. I thought of our last passionate kisses, when we could barely pull ourselves apart. How I longed to phone him, just for a quick fix of his soothing voice but these were the Sixties and only fast girls phoned boys – good girls waited for the phone to ring.

We tried to spend every waking minute together, in between working on our families' farms and other petty annoyances. In my memory most of the days of that summer were splashed with sun; the nights, starlit and romantic. Since Mother still worked at Stockman's, the town's only department store, I milked the cows, pulled weeds from the garden and managed the household. This included keeping Teresa and Terry from physical battles.

Once when I separated them, skinny little Terry shouted, "You think you're such hot stuff just because you're going to the convent. I know what you're doing with Barry in the car. Everybody in Spring Valley does. And don'tcha think God can see you?"

Shouldn't ten-year-old brothers be buried alive until they're sixteen? I resisted the urge to strangle him. How could everyone in Spring Valley know? How could he, for that matter? We always parked under a big old maple at the front of the house. It neatly camouflaged our love bower, or so we thought. Terry's room was at the back of our rambling farmhouse. He couldn't really see us but could he guess?

~ ~ ~

The sweet memories of my last date with Barry clashed with the overhanging cloud of guilt about our impossible future together. How appropriate, then, that what might have been a blissful final summer at home, was underscored by the excruciating pain of my strained back. Oddly enough, the agony that punctuated every movement of the summer was far less memorable than the ecstasy of discovering all there was to know about Barry.

Like the love affair, the back problem started as the summer began.

~ ~ ~

"Hey, Karen," my friend Maggie called as she headed toward my locker a day before exams ended. "Wait up. I hear you've invited all our favourite teachers to your graduation party. Brown-noser! There's no one left for the rest of us to invite." I glanced at her with a little grin. She swung her shiny blonde ponytail in my face – a mild reprimand.

"Why don't you invite Miss Maxwell? You were always her pet," I teased. Our home-ec teacher loved to stand at the top of the stairs in her room and call my classmates over to look at my sewing.

"Now, girls," she'd say sourly, "look at this stitching of Karen's. See how uneven it is? Girls, we don't do that." Someone in the crowd chortled at my misery. "Look, by comparison, at Maggie's work: the stitches are perfectly spaced and neat."

If I ever get to be a teacher, I promised myself, I will never treat kids like that. And I'd never let my hair grow grey and pull it into a severe bun like Maxi-Ann.

"Well, don't keep the faculty all night," Maggie warned. "I want Collins and Ames to put in an appearance at my place after yours." She flicked her golden hair once more to punctuate her remark.

"Gotcha," I grinned and gave that tail a little tug. "Wanna go to the drug store for a lime phosphate? I'm riding home with Mom instead of taking the bus."

"Sure and you can tell me about the valedictory you've written."

Hosting the teachers and relatives meant a thorough spring cleaning for our aging home.

"Maybe we are poor but we don't have to be dirty," Mother said as she and I pulled the old piano out from the wall to make sure the living room was spick-and-span.

"Ohhh," I screamed as a sharp spasm shot through my back.

"What is it? What happened?" Mother asked as we rested the huge beast.

"Uuoooh, my back is killing me. Just let me rest a minute." I leaned against the old upright rubbing my back.

"Sit down over there and I'll deal with the piano myself. Come on."

That was the beginning of debilitating pain. Not all the time. It came and went but it was exacerbated by lifting full cans of milk into the tank of cold water to keep them fresh or handling heavy bales of hay. It definitely wasn't helped by the activities in the driveway in Barry's car.

By mid-July the doctor deemed that the chronically strained back, as he called it, would only get worse if I kept on with this lifestyle. He ordered ten days of complete bed rest in the hospital. It didn't completely heal the back but the change in activities gave me some time to reflect on where things were going. Labour Day was looming and that spelled separation from Barry.

I lay there with my upper body at a forty-five degree angle and my knees bent over a raised hill in the lower bed. This awkward position was meant to remove all the stress from the lower back. I nodded off in drug-induced naps, my troubled brain convinced that the pain was a just punishment for the torrid pleasures of the summer. How could I simply follow my own desires? I remembered Sister Suzanne's promise that the love of God would be returned a hundredfold. I wanted Him to say, Okay, Karen, now you love Me completely, so I'm going to let you have Barry. Just a dream.

Since I spent my late July birthday there, Barry brought my gift to the hospital. The box was small but beautifully packaged. He gave it to me with that shy toss of his head that I found irresistible.

"How lovely!" I exclaimed. "Did you wrap it?"

"No, my mom did but I did pick it out." He hesitated and then said, "It's something that you can use, no matter what you decide to do."

No matter what I decided? God had decided and I didn't have a choice. Remember what Father Riley said? My own desires must be subjugated to this vocation to which I felt so unwillingly called. And I promised Dad, too, didn't I?

I pulled aside the lovely red ribbon and floral print paper to reveal a green velour case containing a manicure set. How inspired. He was right. I could use it anywhere and I really needed one, since fussing with my nails was a low priority. I stretched upward, in spite of the pain, kissing him with a watchful eye on the door lest another visitor or a nurse appear at that instant. His perfect gift would last for many years and bring a sweet recollection of this moment each time I used it.

Finally, released from the hospital I went home, a fragile version of myself. That night after the family went to bed, Barry and I were back on the couch again, cautiously cuddling. For a few more weeks, we could pretend this would last forever.

Once I was on my feet again, Mother decided this was a good time to make the break from Barry. One August Sunday afternoon, she sat in her big chair beside the piano, while I tried to find comfort on the couch. She wore a light plaid shirt and navy blue pedal pushers that she smoothed. She struggled to start this difficult pep talk.

"Don't you think you'd better start tapering off this relationship? After all, people in a small town talk, you know. Everyone's wondering whether you're going to go through with your plans to enter St. Anselm's, including me." Her voice strained to remain calm.

"I'm going; you know I'm going. I don't have a choice, do I? I've been called."

"Of course you still have a choice." Her voice firmer now, she added, "And you'd better start making a final decision. Otherwise, it'll be too late to get into a regular university if you don't enter the convent. You could get a scholarship with your top marks."

"It's already too late. Don't worry," I assured her, "I'm going to St. Anselm's but I do need time to say goodbye to Barry. This is hurting him too." My feet are on the floor now ready to make my escape.

"I know, but the longer you drag it out, the harder it will be. . . for everyone."

"Just leave me alone!" I shouted, stalking off upstairs in tears.

And so, with more than a week to go before we actually had to sever the ties, we said goodbye. We held each other for hours, weeping together, dreaming of worldwide disasters solving the dilemma for us by wiping out the entire universe. Maybe the Russians would actually drop The Bomb. Like young lovers throughout the ages, we thought we were the only people ever to suffer such heartbreak. I traced his face over and over to memorize it. He kissed me on my wet eyelids and I broke into another round of sobbing. He pulled me to him for the last time trying to comfort me. Finally, he walked me to the door, softly kissed me and wished me luck.

"Be sure to let me know if you change your mind," he said. "And call me when you come home for Christmas."

"I will – of course, I will. Maybe we'll run into each other in Eau Claire, since you're going to be at the U."

He looked away, shaking his head. "I don't know whether to hope for that or not – it'll be hard."

"Okay, go now, please go. Goodbye, Barry."

"Goodbye, Karen." I touched his cheek one last time. His eyes pooled with tears, reflecting my own. I stood like a latter day Juliet and watched him go.

He turned without looking back and walked to the car. Through a flood of tears my eyes followed the old green Plymouth as it left the driveway for the last time.

~ ~ ~

There is no question of what we will wear to *Our Town* at the University – our uniforms of black and white were the only wardrobe choice. I loved sharing an extensive wardrobe with my sisters in the past, so it's disappointing to face my persona of the future. I long for Teresa's red dress. What else do I have to wear that is presentable? Hardly the fading skirts and blouses that have now become my Saturday clothes for housecleaning or hiking. Despite this we can at least polish our shoes and primp our hair. Besides, black and white are the perennial colour choices of teenagers, so we're not completely out of fashion. As to the little white collars and cuffs and black bow ties? Not typical. Paula was right. We are indeed a flock of penguins.

We chatter excitedly as we walk the six blocks to the university. It is a warm autumn evening, full of promise. The air smells fresh; the moon is full. How delightful to enter a real auditorium and to have the opportunity to experience some genuine, secular culture. We take our seats with excitement. Eager for the best view, I move to the centre seat. I am as far away from Sister Freda as possible and Sherry is keeping her entertained. We are barely settled when I look up and see a shock of red hair above a very familiar face moving across the row ahead of me. He is going to sit right in front of me. Not Barry but the next best thing – Steve, who is not only another old beau but also Barry's roommate. Steve sees me.

"Karen! My goodness. Good to see you." He leans over to shake my hand and almost whispers, "Does Barry know you're here?"

"Of course not. How could he? It's not as if I can call him."

"My God, I'll go get him. There's an extra seat here. I'll buy it and then call the dorm."

I fidget as I wait for Steve to return. I keep glancing at the entrance to see if he has arrived. Carrying on a conversation with Reenie on my left is impossible. What will he be like? Will he refuse to come? Will he almost ignore me as he once did in high school? Or if he shows an interest, will the others notice it and I end up in trouble with Sister Agnes when she hears? Maybe I'll never be allowed out again.

Five minutes later, Barry enters, improved by absence. He is still running his hand through his hair as he approaches the seat in front of me. His shy smile mixes with wonder that this dreamed-about event is actually happening. His hooded eyes are sleepy and sexy. My heart pounds, my throat closes. I breathe deeply and try to resist perspiring. Memories of those nights in his car in the driveway flash before me. Fantasies of grabbing him and holding him and sharing deep kisses nearly overpower me. Once again I feel that cold sweat creep up my back and over my chest. Oh God, I hope I'm not going to faint again.

As he sits down and we begin to talk, my racing pulse slows a bit and the moment of dizziness passes. What do we say? Does it matter? I only know that we talk until the play begins, all through the intermission and then for a fleeting second after the show ends. Yet even with the distraction of his presence I get caught up in the sad story of Emily and George. Emily's death brings tears to my eyes. I grieve for her untimely end through childbirth. Her attempt to rejoin her old life is heartbreaking. I'm sure their story symbolizes something for me, but my head is too muddled to process it.

As the lights come up and the audience claps, Barry turns once more to me, his eyes tender and concerned.

"Uh, well, I guess, I'd better let you go. Don't want to get you in trouble, or are you already for talking to me?"

With a sideways glance at Sister Freda, I say with some bravado, "Of course not. We can talk to people after all!"

"Okay, then, well, great to see you. I don't know if I'll sleep tonight." He slumps in his seat like a deflated ball.

"Me neither. Well, I'd better go." Our hands brush lightly in something a little more intimate than a handshake. He holds my right one for just a moment.

We go our separate ways. We can't return to our summer romance but it is a sweet moment to savour for those long November nights. Back in my own bed I think of Emily and George, of Barry and Karen, of love and loss.

Chapter VII

A Day In Bed with Bonnie

Sore throat, tight chest, aches all over. Up half the night trying to find relief with water and Aspirin. What else is there in a convent, I grouse? What a lousy day to wake up sick. The splendid sun-streaked days of October have turned into overcast, dreary November. Yet today might have been special. It is a holy day of obligation – All Saints' Day, November 1. The Mass will be very solemn and vibrant; there will be extra singing at the office; the priest will wear his festive cream and gold chasuble; the meals will all be special. Best of all, except in quiet areas like chapel and the halls, silence will be suspended all day. We will be able to talk to the sisters, even the novices. I'd been looking forward to these little treats.

Now here I am, barely able to hold up my head. I hack away as I shower, reminding myself it is one of those things that I should just suffer up, as we've been taught. Then Sherry whispers, "You'd better go back to bed; tell Sister Freda you're sick."

A simple, obvious solution but my brain was too clogged with mucous to think of it myself. I stumble back to the dorm, a wad of Kleenexes in my hand. Sister Freda is already there, bending over Bonnie's bed across the aisle from mine. When she sees me, she turns and says, "Another sicko? Mother of Mercy. You'd better get back in bed; this little one's sick too. And dry that hair; there's nothing worse than being in bed with a wet head." Being sick without my mother maybe? Sister Freda tsk, tsks away, as though I became ill to irritate her. I follow orders and by the time my hair is dry, she is at my cell – pulling back the curtain a little so she can see to take my temperature.

"Both you and Bonnie have mild fevers, so you keep drinking those liquids. We'll bring you some breakfast and then you just rest for the day. You're not going to die, though you'd better remember to say your prayers. My mother, God rest her soul, used to say, 'Plenty of liquids and plenty of prayers.' I don't like that cough of yours though, Karen. I hope it's not going to turn into bronchitis."

I hope not as well. I was rarely ill at home – just the odd cold that seldom kept me away from school, so keen was I to have perfect attendance. I feel a little spoiled being ordered to go back to bed and take care of myself.

We rest. We pick at our breakfasts. We nap till about ten. Although we both think we're being left out of some fun and unusual things, we're too wretched to care. After our nap, we get out of bed, pull back our curtains enough to see each other, crawl back into our beds. Because it is a feast day and the circumstances unusual, we presume permission to talk. This is a liberty we girls love to use to stretch the code of behaviour. When no one is around, we exercise it frequently. We lie back down, then prop up the pillows so we can chat quietly, just in case someone comes in. Bonnie starts to share her life story with me.

"I'm from Chippewa Falls," she says, referring to the town just north of Eau Claire. "And last year, I went to La Crosse to join the Sisters of Notre Dame who teach at my school in

Chippewa, but it just wasn't a good fit for me. For some reason I feel much more at home with the Benedictines. I'm really happy here, aren't you?"

I reflect on this for a moment. Am I happy? I admit it all seems bearable; people are kind, amusing even. Though some rules are rigid and of course, I miss my family and Barry. True, the food and activities are better than I expected. Perhaps it's the fact that it's a unique situation, one my friends and sisters haven't experienced, that makes it pleasant. Am I getting any closer to God? That's what I long for but it's difficult to judge.

I say all this, interrupted occasionally by a tickling cough. She latches onto one factor: "Oh, Barry. A guy. Well, you'd better make up your mind. . ."

"Please don't start sounding like my mother. I know. I know. I'm probably going to stay. I think I have a vocation. So I have to stay, right?"

"Well, that's a pretty negative way to put it. You have to be true to yourself. What feels like the right thing? You don't want to take the veil and then feel you've made a mistake."

"I think this is right. You know what? I saw Barry at the university a couple of weeks ago when we went to see *Our Town*."

She bolts upright, tucked blankets dropping from her chin. "You did? What did you do?" Her schoolgirl interest is clearly piqued.

"Well, his roommate was sitting in front of me, so he left to phone Barry who came right over. We just talked, before and between the play. It was thrilling at the time. Funny, now that I've seen him, I think I can live without him. Still it definitely was amazing to have him appear like that. I don't know. Life's confusing!"

"It is but we all have to cope with these temptations to choose the easy way out. Prayer is the answer. I'll pray for you too, to help you make the right choice."

I look at her in wonder. Here is an offer of friendship. Not just the superficial connections of the other postulants or sisters but someone who understands me and is going to pray for me. Bonnie, a year younger than I am and still attending Regis, is wise beyond her years and exceptionally devout. She is also very placid compared to my kinetic self.

"Thanks, Bonnie." My throat tickles and I undergo another bout of coughing. I choke out a Freda-inspired comment: "Okay, my throat's getting even sorer from all this talking. We'd better rest awhile. Someone will be bringing over some lunch soon, I suppose."

"Yeah. It's good to laze around for a change, isn't it?" She stretches luxuriously. "Let's take advantage of this chance for some extra sleep."

Thinking about temptations and choices keeps me from really resting at first but eventually a sense of peace overwhelms me and I fall into a deep slumber.

~ ~ ~

The days of November fly by as the demands of university courses and religious studies fill our every waking hour. When the frost sets in the area that served as the volleyball court becomes a skating rink. We don heavy sweaters and capes and get some chilling exercise. Rosy-cheeked, we tumble into the kitchen in search of cocoa and cookies, the tummy-warming aromas filling our senses. As usual, Sister Adele is happy to supply this treat as long as we clean up after ourselves.

On December 8th, the feast of the Immaculate Conception, we four postulants – Sherry, Reenie, Paula and I – officially ask to be admitted to the community. For the remainder of the school year, we'll study and practise the Holy

Rule to test whether we truly have vocations. It's curious that the Immaculate Conception is set so close to Christmas. Two miracles! In a small ceremony after Mass, we receive a gold and turquoise medal of our Blessed Mother that we will wear on a black cord around our necks. Classes are cancelled for the day. All the meals are very festive.

Sister Clementine, her face aglow with genuine affection, grabs me around the shoulders as we exit the chapel: "Welcome, Karen; it does my old heart good to receive four enthusiastic new members like you girls into the community."

I choke up having this rough-cut warrior hugging me. Her sentiments are echoed many times that day as the community celebrates its elation. I am almost convinced now that this is my home; this is where I want to be.

When it is time to go to our family homes for the two-week Christmas holiday, I'm surprised I'm not as eager to go as I expected. The younger sisters, especially our driver, Sister Lily and my new role model, Sister Scholastica, are very excited about the things they are going to make as gifts for the person whose name they have drawn. They talk about it after class and I envy them. We postulants are outsiders. Each sister will receive only one gift, so people are highly original in their creations.

What a strange position to be in. Not really at home here or there. Yet. It's time to make up our minds where our hearts belong. The two weeks at home might help us to finalize our decisions. What a wise idea to win us over and then to send us out to get another really good look at the world. My Protestant grandma had suggested they would brainwash us. It doesn't feel like that. I can't speak for anyone else but I know which way I am leaning.

Chapter VIII

Christmas on the Farm

Of course it is good to be home, I tell myself. Except that after four months enjoying sleeping alone in my single bed, I'm back in the double one I've always shared with Teresa, telling her convent tales late into the night. At least she's interested. Over meals Terry listens with one ear. Now nine-years-old, he is meeting his buddies in the nearby tiny village of Olivet – reduced to a school and a store with a crumbling church up the hill – to play board games, or to watch cowboy shows on TV. Mother is glad to have me home to help prepare for Christmas. The tree is already trimmed when I get home with presents piled beneath. I'm in time to help with the cookie baking and the special holiday cleaning. Lucky me.

Being at home brings back memories of Dad. Glancing out the kitchen window the morning after my arrival home, my lip quivers as I watch the milkman drive in. Is it Mike, who was a buddy of Dad's? No, a new one. Tears well as I recall Christmas three years ago.

~ ~ ~

Dad glanced out the kitchen window as the milk truck plowed through the driveway, its heavy tires breaking a path through fresh snow. Despite the holiday, the milkman made his appointed rounds. Dad seized the opportunity to have his first drink of the day. As soon as Mike drove up the knoll from the milk house capped by six new inches of eider down, Dad was on the porch, waving him into the house. The faded red barn surrounded by snow banks looked like a scene from Currier and Ives.

"Merry Christmas, Mike," Dad yelled. "Come in and have a little cheer."

Mike leaned his long face out of the half-open window.

"I dunno, Don. I've got the rest of my route to finish."

"Aw, c'mon, it's Christmas. Just one quick little drink."

"All right." Mike nodded. He didn't act surprised. The farmers in this part of Wisconsin were friends of his family from way back. A wee snort or two was a highlight of every occasion.

As Mike exited the truck that he'd pulled close to the house, Dad pumped his hand.

"Careful on the porch step," Dad warned, gesturing. "Needs fixing. Guess it'll have to wait till spring though. Too damn cold for outdoor carpentry."

"You got that right," Mike said, gingerly avoiding the hazardous step. "Don, I really shouldn't drink on the route. Maybe coffee?"

"Nah, it's Christmas," Dad insisted. He was always glad to have someone to drink with.

They entered the kitchen, their breaths fogging the windows of the door. Mike meekly removed his dark cap and unzipped his heavy wool plaid jacket. He nodded to Mother and me as we peeled potatoes over the sink.

"Edie, a couple of glasses and the peppermint schnapps," Dad ordered.

"Get it yourself, Donny. I'm busy fixing Christmas dinner. Hi, Mike; sit down and have some of those cookies on the table."

"Thanks," Mike said, helping himself with one bony hand. His face was unshaven. He was not a Catholic, so he hadn't been to midnight Mass as we had. No doubt he'd clean up later.

"Mmm. Smells good in here, Edie. That turkey must be nearly finished," Mike declared.

"Well, we plan to eat around twelve-thirty. It's been in since seven this morning"

The meal would be a feast. No matter how tough things were, there was always plenty of food. The counters were covered with candied sweet potatoes, pans of peas and beans, waiting to be baked or cooked. In the refrigerator were cranberry sauce and a couple of Jell-o salads.

I glanced around at the tired old kitchen. Sure could use a coat of paint. The pea-green walls were grayed with oil furnace residue. Now the men had tracked in wet snow on the clean floor. I shook my head. So hard to keep an old house clean.

Dad patted Mom lightly on her broad butt as he passed her en route from the cupboard with the schnapps and the glasses. She sighed. "There's no point in nagging him," she whispered to me. "Christmas is a better excuse for him to drink than most days." She kept peeling potatoes and tried her best to ignore the second drink he poured for himself. Occasionally, she wiped her hand on the festive apron worn over a good wash dress. She'd made both herself of fabric from the clothing store, not the flour sack material she often salvaged. Her dark hair was neatly permed and pinned out of the way.

"Have another, Mike, a drink the colour of a Christmas tree. Down the hatch," Dad said, topping up his glass. Dad's cheeks were already rosy, a shade lighter than his wavy auburn hair. "Why don't you get another one of the big girls to help you, Edie?"

"Rita did help but I told her to take a rest. You know I can't work very well with too many people under foot."

As if on cue, our old brown and white dog, Pal, entered the kitchen from the dining room. He smelled like the wet mutt that he was.

"Go on, now, Pal, shoo," Mother yelled, kicking at the air. "Terry, come and take this dog out of here."

Sitting in the dining room doorway, Terry dropped the new toy truck he was playing with, his best gift from Santa and plodded into the kitchen.

"Hey, little man," Dad said grabbing him and taking him into his lap, "just because you're only seven doesn't mean you can sit around in your pajamas all day. Grandma Rodewald and Uncle Earl will be here in an hour or so."

The pretty boy with curly ash-blond locks rubbed his eyes in tired confusion. Along with the rest of us, he'd worshipped at midnight Mass last night. Santa arrived while we were gone, so Terry hadn't had much sleep.

"But I'm s'posed to keep Pal out of the kitchen. I don't know what to do first."

"That's okay, Terry, just get Pal out of here. Then have Karen help you get dressed. Come on, everyone has to give me a hand today." Mother's voice was strained.

I wiped my hands, glad to get out of kitchen chores for a few minutes.

Dad helped by pouring himself another glass of schnapps.

"More for you, Mike?"

"Nah, I'd better get back to work. Besides," he said, winking at Dad in collusion, "I'm sure I'm underfoot too."

Rattled, Mother assured him, "Oh, no, Mike, I didn't mean you."

"That's all right. Gotta go. Merry Christmas!" Grabbing his cap, he left. A final blast of cold air followed his departure.

"No more schnapps now, Don. It's only 10:00 in the morning. Remember your diabetes, if nothing else."

"Don't start!"

"Don't you start! Go play with the kids."

Dad lumbered out of the kitchen mumbling, "No point in spoiling Christmas."

I watched him wander into the dining room. I shook my head sadly. Why did he have to drink, I asked myself for the thousandth time. I'd heard stories of women who dropped a blessed medal in their husbands' coffee, removed it and soon the men gave up alcohol. I wondered if such a miracle were possible but feared I'd be caught in the act.

At eleven, my older brother Jim and his wife Sandy arrived, loaded down with two babies and all their paraphernalia: Tracie, a mere fourteen months old and Tony, barely three weeks. I rushed to grab Tony from Sandy. My three sisters, Rita, Maureen and Teresa were close at hand to fight over this precious bundle.

"What a big beautiful boy you are," I said nuzzling him. He smells like a baby, pure and powdered.

"I want the baby," Rita insisted.

"I asked first."

"Oh, Karen, you're always pushing yourself to the head of the line. C'mon, Tracie, come to Aunt Rita." Rita whipped her long dark hair defiantly and took Tracie from Jim.

I swallowed Rita's unseasonal criticism and headed to the living room rocking chair with little Tony who woke to the sound of his aunts' skirmish. The living room was the most festive in the house with a large tree spilling into most of the space. A few wrapped gifts remained under it.

Rita led Tracie to the Christmas tree and squatted to help her find a gift with her name on it.

"Twee," she said, pointing proudly.

"Wow, Tracie, not only can you walk but you can talk!" Rita says.

"Doggie," she said, patting Pal, who parked near the tree.

Her aunts cheered her on. "Daddy," she added, pointing to Jim as he entered and helped Teresa spread their gifts under the tree.

Exhaustion lined Jim's handsome face. Lack of sleep, no doubt. He nodded to everyone and collapsed on the couch beside Maureen.

From the rocking chair in the living room, I watched Uncle Earl drive in; his dark blue Chev was clean as always, sparkling against the snow. In a couple of minutes he and Grandma entered the kitchen. Mother let them in.

"Hi, Ma and Earl," I heard Mother shout and I imagined her giving them quick hugs. "Just put your coats over there on our bed and join the rest in the living room. I've gotta get back to the dinner."

"Grandma! Uncle Earl." A chorus of greetings ensued with a more subdued "Lena, Earl," from Dad. Grandma was short and slowed down by arthritis, or "Arthur" as she called it. Her commentaries on Arthur peppered her conversation: "I've got it so bad in my knees" or "I've got it so bad in my neck."

Grandma frowned at Dad as she gave him a hug. Smelling the schnapps on his breath, she waved her hand in front of her nose. "Already been nipping at the bottle, have you?" she said. He ignored her.

Earl wandered around, arms behind his back, looking at everything, saying little. Then he grabbed his cigarettes and Dad remembered what he had in common with this brother-in-law. They sat on the old couch in the dining room, smoking quietly. The wallpaper, once beige, was now a dreary tan in spots water-soaked from leaks. A picture of Jesus pointing to His Sacred Heart hung above the buffet.

In a little while, before Dad could start offering pre-dinner drinks, Mother put everyone to work. She stood in the living room archway and announced to both rooms: "Now I could use some help. Donny, in a few minutes you can carve, Rita and Maureen, you can help me dish out, Jim and Earl, get that extra leaf into the table. Then Karen and Teresa, you can cover the tables with those linen tablecloths from my third dresser drawer and set the table with the china and silverware. It's Christmas and we've got 'em, so we might as well use 'em."

Once we sat down Dad led us in prayer: "Bless us, oh Lord and these thy gifts, which we are about to receive from Thy bounty, through Christ our Lord. Amen." Even Grandma and Earl, Protestant though they were, repeated the "amen." Then everyone dived into the appetizing feast, scooping large portions on their plates and passing the platters and bowl to the right.

"I got the wishbone," Teresa exclaimed and Terry screeched, "It was my turn for it."

"Now, now, don't start a battle today. You can wish together after Teresa's finished with it," Mother intervened.

Mollified, Terry grabbed some slices of breast.

For a time, everyone ate quietly, savouring the festive meal. I scooped a second helping of stuffing onto my plate, though I realised I'd be too full for dessert. I couldn't resist my favourite dish, served only on special occasions.

While the adults and older kids sipped their Mogen David, a cheap and over-sweet wine bought for special occasions, I stuck to milk like Teresa and Terry.

Sitting at one end of the table with Maureen at my right and Dad at the end on my left, I kept an eye on the way the large bottle emptied. When it was gone, Dad held it up and looked into it sadly, a lost friend. Mom hustled the empty bottle out to the kitchen along with some bowls now scraped clean by the hungry crowd. But Dad found another he'd hidden in a cupboard.

Sandy was busy with her children before dinner, so after the main course, she gave the baby to Jim and went to the kitchen to make grasshoppers for everyone. I watched her hold up the bottle of schnapps, assessing how much Dad left. Fortunately, there was plenty.

Everyone else was almost too full to talk but Grandma turned to Rita and asked, "How do you like your job and apartment in the Twin Cities?"

"Oh, it's great. I like living on my own in St. Paul and the Minneapolis insurance company is a fun place to work."

Dad looked at her raising his chin and giving his head a shake, "I hope that Logan fella isn't spending nights there with you."

Rita blushed. "Dad, don't embarrass me in front of the whole family. And his name is Wayne, not that Logan fella."

"Well, you just keep your legs crossed; in fact, that goes for all of you girls."

"What do you mean, Dad?" Teresa, only eleven, scrunched her innocent face.

"Oh, you'll find out soon enough. Just remember what I said." He pours himself and the other adults another round of wine. I tried it once since Dad offered it now that I'm fifteen, but it was terrible. Why would anyone want to drink wine? It seemed to make Dad happy. If only he could stop with just a little, but he never did. I could see he was beginning to nod. Any minute now, he might fall asleep where he sat.

"What are you going to do after you graduate, Maureen?" Grandma asked. "I don't see you older girls much since you got to be teenagers. Only Teresa and Terry ever stay with me anymore."

"Oh, I plan to go to college in River Falls in September. Probably be an elementary teacher. Though I also like the idea of nursing, like Aunt Mimi," Maureen replies.

"Well, there are plenty of teachers on both sides of the family, too," Mother put in, "and teachers will never have to worry about finding work."

"I'm going to do that, too, Grandma," I piped up before Maureen could say anything more. "I want to teach high school English. But Dad would like it if I'd become a nun." Maureen shook her head at my interruption.

Grandma frowned. "Karen, what a terrible waste of your brain. And you are too spunky to be locked away someplace you can't talk or see people." Then with a quick glance at him, she whispered, "And what does your dad know about it anyway?"

"Grandma, have you ever been to a convent? It's not really that bad. Since you're not Catholic, it probably doesn't make much sense to you, but. . ."

Sandy entered the dining room with a trayful of grasshoppers. Maureen jumped up to help. Dad woke from his half-doze and eyed Sandy's tall slim figure nodding.

"You sure thinned out in a hurry after the baby."

"Donald, that's your daughter-in-law. Show some respect," Mother chided.

"Jesus Christ, don't yell at me. It was a compliment."

Jim, both sleep-deprived and stuffed from the heavy meal, roused himself to say, "Just leave Mom alone, Dad."

Dad leapt up, his face red with anger. He reeled a bit. Mother held her breath. Tony started to bawl and Sandy took him, cuddling him, carrying him upstairs to breastfeed. Tracie held out her arms to Jim. He pulled her onto his lap and she snuggled under her dad's chin.

"Maybe, you'd better have a little nap before Santa comes, Donny." Mom's voice sounded as if she were soothing a child. "When you're ready, Santa's things are in the woodshed."

Dad's rotund figure would fit the Santa costume without padding. If he woke up in time to play his role.

"Yeah, I'll have a li'l nap," he slurs. "I shouldn't drink those sweet things anyway. Bothers my diabetes."

"It don't look to me as if you're very worried about your diabetes," Grandma snarled.

Dad just waved, too sleepy to start another round, headed into the downstairs bedroom off the dining room and closed the door.

After dishes were finished I headed up to Teresa's and my bedroom for a nap – a chance to get away from the confusion below and to begin reading one of my favourite Christmas gifts, *Jane Eyre*. I couldn't rest. I revisited the unfinished conversation about my plans for going to the convent. Part of me wanted to fulfill my destiny, if that's what it was, and to get an inexpensive university education. The other part wished Barry Nelson would finally realize that I was the girl for him. I turned back to *Jane Eyre*, whose life was also marked by difficult choices.

~ ~ ~

I must have dozed off. I awoke to the commotion downstairs and Teresa calling me, "Karen, Santa's here."

Sure enough, Dad was neatly decked out in Santa's clothes. His drink-bloomed cheeks were the right colour and the outfit, a perfect fit. He handed out the gifts left under the tree, plus a few small ones from his bag.

Terry wasn't convinced. "You're not Santa," he laughed, "you're Dad! You smell just like my dad. Like peppermint candy."

"Shhh! "Dad laid a finger against his lips. "Don't tell Tracie that. Come here, Tracie, come sit on Santa's knee."

She shyly sucked her two fingers, then wiped them on her pretty red corduroy dress. "Papa? Papa?"

We all laughed. Dad hadn't fooled anyone.

"I guess there's no point in you dressing up next year, Don. Unless Tony hasn't figured it out," Mom cajoled.

"Too bad. I like the costume and I wish I had more to give away here." Santa looked a bit sheepish.

I hoped he wasn't going to get maudlin now that he was starting to sober up after his nap.

"It's okay, Dad, we all have each other. That's enough," I said.

He handed out a few more gifts, then Santa made his exit. After a few minutes, Dad came in from the woodshed with the same rosy cheeks as St. Nick.

~ ~ ~

Christmas day was finally over. A relief – I could see it on Mother's face. She collapsed in her rocking chair, her head lolling to one side. She could barely keep her pale blue eyes open. The company was gone, food stored, kids' toys stashed away, and no real catastrophes to mark the day. The gifts weren't big, expensive ones – mostly clothes and books for "the big kids," a little sewing machine for Teresa, an Erector set and trucks for Terry. But things had improved since Mother started working at the store. At least she didn't have to scrimp on food anymore and the staff discount on clothing helped to stretch the dollar.

Too much of Dad's income didn't make it home. Spring Valley, Wisconsin, population 995, had five churches and six bars. A lot of temptations for a sociable Irishman like him. He was snoring loudly in the bedroom; no loud quarrels erupted all day – something to be thankful for. I uttered a silent prayer that he would not be drinking by next Christmas.

Wishes have a strange way of coming true.

~ ~ ~

Dad's not the only one missing from the farm this Christmas. Rita and Wayne are married and Maureen works extra hours at the nursing home but I am eager to see her. She lives in a house with three other girls in River Falls. On Friday Mom says, "Why don't you take me to work at noon, then take the car to pick her up after she finishes work this afternoon? She's off until tomorrow night. You can have a nice long visit."

"Great idea."

So I drive the twenty miles to the busy university town where Maureen is studying and working. It is exhilarating to be behind the wheel again after not driving for four months. I feel released from something – outside those wrought iron gates and freed from the oppression of silence. I'm snug in a favourite sweater and slacks, a pleasant change. The roads are a little slippery with blowing and drifting snow but I have things under control. This new car of Mom's handles so well. It's her pride and joy, her first large purchase after Dad's death. "I've never had to dicker for a car before," she said. "Your dad always did that." I feel a great responsibility driving it.

Just at the edge of town, the traffic begins to slow down as the volume increases. Suddenly, I hear a loud bang and my car flies forward, striking the car ahead. Dear God, I hit that lady's car! Wait – my mom's new car is now wrapped around a utility pole, completely bashed in. I've wrecked Mom's car! I burst into tears. Within seconds, someone opens the door on the driver's side; it is undamaged.

"Are you all right?" the man asks.

Barely able to answer in my grief I finally manage to blubber, "I think so, except that my neck hurts."

"Probably whiplash. Not surprising. That idiot in the truck behind you slammed into your car and pushed you into the car ahead. Then you skidded sideways and hit the utility pole. Thank God, you didn't have a passenger. Anyone in this seat," he gestures to the passenger side, "would be dead." Oh Lord,

Teresa had nearly come along. Relief washes over me and I burst into tears again.

"There, there, the police are here now. Is there anyone that you want me to call?"

I sputter out our home phone number where Teresa can take the message. I can barely remember it. Teresa will call Maureen and Mother. I won't have to break the news to anyone. I sit in the damaged car in a daze.

The afternoon is a blur of telling my story to the police, of Maureen and her friend arriving to comfort and help me. How wonderful to leave all the paper work in my big sister's hands. She takes me to the hospital to be x-rayed – yes, just whiplash – then she phones the insurance agent. Finally, all the trivia of a near-death experience being sorted out, Maureen's friend drives us home to the farm. When we pick up Mother at the store, she and I both dissolve in tears.

"I'm so sorry, Mom. I know you loved that car. I was driving so carefully and. . . "

"Oh, for heaven's sake, Karen, it's only a car. We can get another one but we can't replace you. Thank God you weren't hurt worse than you are."

"Thanks, Mom." Her expression of love warms me. I'm sure she's worried about replacing the car but she doesn't show it. Even though it wasn't my fault, I'm racked with guilt. I probably don't deserve her kindness, but I'm grateful for it.

~ ~ ~

Somehow, keeping busy to make up for the accident, I get through the days leading up to Christmas. It is a joyful occasion with the growing family gathered. Rita and Wayne now have two sons, Todd and Perry, and Jim and Sandy have another boy, Tim. For today at least the house is full.

Mother continues the tradition of a drink for the milkman but doesn't indulge herself. Of course, we are still getting used to trying to celebrate without Dad. During holidays so many little things reopen the wounds of his loss. Even if he didn't always behave himself, we loved him dearly.

My thoughts keep turning back to my sisters at St. Anselm's and imagining the beauty of their holiday with all the rituals and colour. Here everything seems chaotic with so much coming and going of relatives. There is hardly time to concentrate on the religious mysteries as I find myself longing to do.

Chapter IX

Bride of Christ

The humane piety of the nuns, the richness of the liturgy and the encouragement of my colleagues have helped me come to a decision. I know now I have to make a final call to Barry.

He picks up right away, as if he's been waiting by the phone.

"How are you?" I fight the conflicting emotions of moving to finality.

"I'm okay but what about you? I heard you were in a car wreck last week."

"Yes, I suffered a little whiplash, but I'm okay. Sadly, Mom's new car was totalled. The insurance will cover it though." I pause a second. "How did you hear about the accident?"

"Someone told me about it at Hersey last Friday."

Hersey? The rotten wretch. He'd gone to Hersey – our place – found out about my accident and didn't even call? It hurts that he doesn't want me, even though I'm the one ending it. Didn't he really care at all? I force down my rising anger and mull over his apparent indifference. It makes the next sentence so much easier to say: "I've decided to stay at St. Anselm's."

A beat. Then, "I figured you would. I could tell already in October that you were settling in there." His voice lacks emotion.

"The convent seems right to me now. It's – I don't know – like living on another plane, away from the distractions of the world. I feel as if I belong there."

He makes no effort to dissuade me – the creep. Instead he says, "Well, I'm glad you weren't hurt. Have a good life. See you sometime."

Is this the dream man for whom I was prepared to throw over my commitment to Christ?

This is so much easier than it had been in August.

"Yeah, you too." My voice is dead. "goodbye."

~ ~ ~

The events of the Christmas holidays sharpen my appreciation for St. Anselm's, so I settle back with increased fervour into the preparations for becoming a novice. Yvonne did not return from her home after Christmas. She couldn't bear to spend so much time away from her family. It's a sad reality. Finding that this life is not for you is as important as discovering you can make the commitment. There's no right or wrong – it's a personal choice. I wish her well. At least she learned to make a bed with hospital corners.

On the next family visiting day, Sherry's father, who has become a surrogate dad to me, starts calling me "Sister Fender Bender," as a result of my accident. The word spreads and even before I've got a veil, I have a Sister nickname. I'm not pleased with it, but I laugh it off and say nothing.

Bonnie influences my growing devotion. She is younger than I, yet wiser in many ways. I watch her devotion at prayer, her contemplative manner and try to emulate it. I also admire the charming and ebullient Sister Scholastica and chat with her during breaks between classes whenever I can. "My baptismal name is Bridget but Mother Dorothy prefers that we change our names – to complete our turning to God and to help us forget our past."

"Bridget, I've always loved that name. It sounds so Irish, which was my Dad's background. I'm thinking of taking it when I become a nun in June. Would you mind?"

"I'd be honoured," Sister Scholastica says. "Now tell me about your topic for the next speech in Sister Jeanette's class."

~ ~ ~

More and more St. Anselm's feels like the right choice – this does seem to be the life for me. These people combine piety and humanity; why can't I?

My courses continue to go well. I love the rich combination of secular and religious studies. Now the focus is on becoming a novice. Sister Agnes explains in our postulant class: "Your acceptance into the community, or reception, as we call it, will occur on June 21, in St. Patrick's church in Eau Claire. It's a lot like a wedding, so you can invite your family and friends. You will wear bridal gowns to enter the church. Then a series of rituals will mark the changes in your lives."

"What about the tonsure?" Paula asks. "Are they really going to shave our heads with only that little bit of hair left?"

"I'm coming to that, Paula. After some opening prayers, the bishop will remove your veils, one by one and perform the tonsure. It will not be the full shaving of the top of the head, surrounded by a ring of hair as the monks used to wear, since your hair will soon be covered by headgear. This haircut is designed to symbolize the way the young sister is dedicating her natural beauty to Christ. Then the Bishop will whisper the names by which you will be known 'in religion' and hand you a complete habit to take behind the altar for redressing.

"As I think I mentioned a couple of weeks ago, you are allowed to make a couple of choices. Have you made up your minds yet?"

"Yes, Sister, I would like to be either Sister Faith or Sister Hope," Sherry says.

"I see," Sister Agnes nods with a twinkle. "How virtuous. Anyone else?"

Paula and Reenie both shake their heads. "I'm still thinking," Reenie comments. Paula nods in agreement.

"I would like to be either Sister Kathleen or Sister Bridget. Here's my written list for Mother Dorothy," I say.

"Well, Karen," Sister Agnes says, "we had a Sister Kathleen in the community. She worked in the Eau Claire area for years and was very well known. Unfortunately, she left the community a couple of years ago, so I think people in town might be confused if her name reappears so soon. You'd better talk to Mother Dorothy directly."

When I have the chance a couple of days later, Mother agrees with Sister Agnes' view about the name Kathleen. "But you'd be happy with Bridget?" she asks.

"Oh, yes, Mother," I say with delight. "In fact, that was my first choice."

"Well, then, it should be yours." She glances again at my paper. "This spelling is the Swedish saint, not the Irish one. The Irish one is Brigid. Did you realize that?"

"Oh, no, I had been trying to celebrate my Irish heritage but it really doesn't matter much anyway which saint will be looking out for me. Bridget seems easier to say than Brigid, if that doesn't sound strange."

"I know what you mean. Karen, you've got a positive

outlook which is good. You're just the kind of person this community needs." I redden at her praise and thank her. The sisters are all so encouraging. Deep affection for them floods me.

~ ~ ~

Reception Day is a perfect June wedding day – the air fragrant with mock orange blossoms, the brilliant sun and light breeze accentuate our mood of optimism. We four postulants look stunning in the shimmering white satin gowns that Sister Freda made us, all alike except for the sizes. Cummerbunds bind our slim waists. On our heads are little crowns with sheer veils attached.

We're allowed to see our families before the ceremony; we even have breakfast together. I have to be very careful not to spill anything on my gown. Outside St. Patrick's church we take many pictures of the event with various family groupings. When we hug goodbye before the service, we know that although we'll be able to celebrate again after the investiture, life will never be remotely the same. Of course, my family will always be nearest and dearest to me but now I am truly joining our Benedictine family. In many ways that matter, they will take precedence from now on. It is a bittersweet moment.

Mom looks splendid in the silvery blue outfit that she wore for Jim's wedding with her straw hat trimmed in navy blue ribbon. It was difficult for her to get the day off, since this event occurs mid-week though she doesn't let on. Teresa tells me privately. I am sad but not surprised. Her boss, whom we dubbed Simon Legree, has no sense of the importance of occasion. She missed our Christmas concerts and other events because he apparently needed her at work more than we did.

Nearly everyone I invited is here and decked out in their finest: all my siblings – Jim and Sandy with their kids, Rita, who is pregnant again, Maureen, Teresa and Terry – aunts, uncles, cousins, grandmas, a few friends and former priests.

I miss my dad at this moment. He wouldn't have been giving me away as in a typical wedding but it's an important occasion. A wave of sadness washes over me. He would have been so proud. Then I smile at those who are here. It really does feel like a wedding. Like a bride, I am nervous and excited – though exhausted, as I have hardly slept all night.

The altar and celebrants are decked out in white and gold. This is a momentous day for the Church as well as for the postulants and their families. Every new servant of Christ is a welcome addition to God's army. The Bishop, resplendent in cape and mitre, is the major celebrant. He leads the high Mass, surrounded by all the priests that we have invited, other "soldiers of the cross." Fathers Riley, Muzarka and Galt are here for me – the men whom I have observed from earliest childhood as they performed the works of God.

My throat grows dry as the time of the Offertory approaches, for that is the moment in the Mass when we will be officially welcomed into our new community. Memories of Barry compete with snatches of dreams of my future as a nun. We brides of Christ stand in a semicircle around the altar each with our private thoughts about our approaching fate.

When it is time for me to kneel before the bishop as he stands with scissors poised, I weep. Clip, clip, a few swift snips and brown curls drop to the floor. Since he has grabbed the handiest locks, from the crown, I must look a bit weird, indeed like the monks with their tonsures. "Karen Louise Traynor, henceforth you will be known in religion as Sister Mary Bridget, OSB." He hands me the folded habit and veil and I make my way to the sacristy, fighting tears all the way. My joy battles with my sense of loss.

Sister Scholastica is waiting to dress me. This intimate task will cement our friendship. First, Sister Myra, the novice mistress, is ready with some scissors of her own. She deftly flips a large towel around my shoulders in the style of a practised beautician.

"We'll just take a little more hair off the sides now, so it doesn't stick out of your coif. Then we'll give you a proper haircut tonight."

Chop, chop! Hack, hack! I watch as more curls, so carefully coifed for the occasion, sully the polished sacristy floor. I want to be happy in this moment but losing my hair – it's too much to bear. I always spent so much time fussing with it, and even more so on this, its "last day." Sacrificing my hair for the love of Christ rankles like a punishment. Sister Myra dusts off the loose hairs. Then Sister Scholastica begins to remove my white wedding dress and to place the black habit over me for the first time. From glowing bride to subdued nun in one fell swoop. My days of colourful clothes are gone – another sacrifice for my Bridegroom who wants me all to himself. The habit is a simple design – good serge with wide pleats which fall neatly into place, then the elastic black cincture which holds it all in. Next the pleats are straightened. A prayer accompanies each of these, asking God to help me become his temple. Now a little white skullcap is placed on my head. It fits snugly. Over that the crisp pleated coif is pulled on to frame my face. Once pinned to the skullcap, a French braid is made of the ends of the coif and it is pinned again. It feels tight but Sister Scholastica assures me, "You don't want it too loose; you'll have to worry about it falling off when you're doing all that talking with your family." I test it, opening and closing my jaw a few times, and the flat part of the coif wobbles like a duck's bill. A starched white band is placed on the crown of my head and pinned to the top of the coif. A fresh-smelling small under-veil, followed by a perfectly ironed and folded, brand new white veil completes the outfit with a white hatpin on top. I'm sure I look great. I just manage to sneak a peek in the sacristy mirror before Sister Myra reminds me: "Sister," she warns gently, "you are now dead to the world and its vanities." Okay, maybe but I still want to look good when I go back out there in front of all those guests.

One by one, my three classmates join me behind the sacristy, our faces a mixture of elation and sadness. Sherry is now Sister Faith; Reenie, Sister Monique; Paula, Sister Francesca – a lot for everyone to remember.

We struggle to maintain a respectful sense of decorum for the occasion, to avoid exchanging tales of the conflicting emotions of the moment. Between Sister Myra and our dressers, there are enough good influences to encourage us to remain appropriately solemn, though I can't help sneaking a glance at Sherry – Sister Faith – as her head bends to the chopping block, just as mine bent moments before.

Finally, four new novices, led by Sister Myra, return to the altar, where the Bishop presents us to our guests. What a shock and thrill it must be for our loved ones to see us as nuns, no longer the girls they knew, nor the quasi-brides we'd been only minutes before. My stomach is tied in knots so I take a deep breath and try to remember that I am Christ's representative now. I slide my hands under my scapular, straighten my back and bow my head in the perfect decorum that Sister Agnes taught us.

The day is full of celebrations. Once we are outside St. Patrick's, having followed the long procession of bishop, priests and the entire community, we novices are the centre of attention, the heart of the reception line. Mother Dorothy enfolds each of us to her bosom, followed by Sister Cecilia and crusty old Sister Clementine. Our families stand off to the side. Observing the joy evinced by the community at gaining four new young members perhaps helps them to deal with their sense of loss. Yes, we are still theirs but now in a detached way. They've sacrificed too.

Back at the Priory the community honours us with a sumptuous luncheon served outdoors in the bright sunshine. Knowing that we won't see even our families until Christmas, six months away, we take advantage of the opportunity to catch up on all the news and to anticipate coming events, such as Rita's baby expected in November.

Our guests stay until late afternoon, when it is time for the special Vespers and Compline to celebrate the occasion. Our farewells are a little teary but we are more settled than ten months ago when we entered St. Anselm's. I put on a brave face for my family. We can still write despite the separation. Our ties with the world are being gently loosened. Even our birthdays will no longer be celebrated, except, we hope, by our families. Now we will celebrate our name days on the feast of our Patron saints, in my case, October 8th for St. Bridget of Sweden. When I wave goodbye this time, I feel full of love of my new life and family, not the loss I felt last September.

Chapter X

The Corner Turned

The community's gift to each of us is a brand new breviary; it contains the complete Divine Office. The new pages stick gently together and the fresh inky scent of the unused book emanates from them as we pray Vespers and Compline with the community for the first time as nuns.

After prayers, we four new novices follow the line of sisters to the formal dining room for our first meal there with the community. We are shown to our seats; I am next to Sister Krista, a novice who will soon take first vows. On my other side is Sister Faith. Because of the special occasion, silence is again suspended. We find ourselves a part of an excited and noisy crowd who can hardly maintain their usual decorum. I keep waiting for Sister Agnes to say, "Sisters, modulate your voices!"

I sigh but can't stop smiling. It feels right. Good choice, I muse. Now that wasn't so hard was it? As we finish Matins, the final prayers of the day, and kneel to say goodnight to our new bridegroom, contentment fills my soul. All my uncertainties of the past year vanish as I ascend the stairway to the novitiate on the third floor.

Novices are supposed to be separated from the rest of the community as much as possible. In this relatively small house, that is a challenge. We have to walk past the other sisters on the stairs as we ascend or descend. It's one of the main reasons for building a larger Motherhouse, especially since the community is growing quickly.

We walk into the dimly lit dormitory with its eight beds, covered with similar spreads to those at Benet Hall, except these are blue. The three senior novices quickly set about closing the curtains around their cells. Soon their shadows play upon the white dividers. Then Sister Myra calls us four young women into her office, just to the right of the dormitory entrance.

It is a stark room, both a bedroom and command centre. A single bed covered with a basic white spread is in the far corner. The desk's role is clearly more central. Made of oak, it is a handsome piece; its top is neatly organized. A framed prayer card to Saint Jude, the patron of hopeless causes, is on the left side. I wonder how many of her past and present novices fit that description.

To the right of the door, Sister Myra opens the large cupboard holding the supplies such as soap, toothpaste, deodorant and sanitary napkins, which she will dole out to the novices as we need them. On the left side of the middle shelf is an electric clipper. My heart sinks as she selects it along with a clean black comb.

Sister Myra waves the clipper in our direction as she beckons us closer. "Now, are you all feeling okay?"

Naturally, we nod, though looking at that clipper, I am not so sure.

"Well," she says in a sprightly manner, "it's going to be a hot summer and novices have to do a lot of the manual labour, like laundry and coif-making. It takes its toll, especially as you will just be getting used to all these hot clothes. So I recommend that you let me give you a proper haircut. You'll be a lot more comfortable and you don't have to worry about your hair sticking out of your coifs all the time, the way Sister Monique's is doing now." Reenie blushes at hearing her new name and being singled out for not keeping her hair under control.

"I'm not picking on you, Sister Monique; tonight it's you, tomorrow, it could be one of the others. I'm not forcing you to get a real haircut but I'm recommending it," she says evenly. I glance at her face, lit with a smile and put my trust in her benevolence.

"Okay, I'm willing," I say, since I assume Sister Myra will simply make the rough cut neater. I stand before her, biting my tongue, ready to practise obedience. With the clipper she buzzes across my pretty brown hair. BZZT, BZZT, BZZT! – like a swarm of angry bees. In a matter of minutes, she nearly shaves my head. It is the cut commonly called "the Heinie." Were its sporters lookalikes of German soldiers? Shocked and upset, I weep. The falling clumps of hair stick to my damp cheeks. The others weep in sympathy but Sister Myra chirps, "Now that's better. Let's do it to all of you."

With wonderful camaraderie my classmates offer their own heads and soon the four of us look like army conscripts – a grim scene. What a brilliant way to make sure we don't turn tail and run, at least not for a few months until our hair grows back. Only if we bump into someone as we come out of the shower, will anyone see our hair for a long time. It seems in Marc Antony's words, "the most unkindest cut of all." But it is a way of proving to Christ that I truly mean to be His bride and no one else's. On the outside at least, I am dead to the world.

Chapter XI

Challenged by Vanity

Now that the ceremony of reception is behind us, we are no longer stars of any show. Overnight we have become the village drudges. I wipe the sweat from my brow with a bared forearm while I mangle sheets. I feed the folded fabric between the two power-driven cylinders and the steam rises as the sheets are pressed. As a postulant I wondered who was ironing all of our bed linens. Now I know. The smell of soap powder tickles my nose. Sister Myra constantly reminds us of the benefits of "mortifying the flesh," learning to deal with discomfort without complaining. It requires a lot of self-discipline at times. Most of the manual labour falls to the novices and a great deal of it is hot and tiresome.

We feed a hundred sheets a week through the mangle. The vapour from the hot damp linens permeates our pores and mixes with streams of sweat. Our habits are very hot; there is no air-conditioning. Learning to mortify the flesh is a lesson that I hope will end soon. Tee shirts under the habit need frequent changing. It's very hard to get rid of that noisome odour of perspiration no matter how much we soak them in vinegar. God sent us a hot, humid summer with little wind or rain to give us any reprieve.

Good thing we can't talk much. Sister Myra frequently reminds us that this is an excellent way for us to make up for all the sins of our own past lives, as well as those of the rest of the world. Sweat on!

The old novices teach us these chores and from their gleeful grins we can tell they are only too happy to be passing the torch. One labour Sister Mina loves is mowing the lawn – getting good exercise, being outdoors and relishing the occasional breeze. For her it is a solitary effort with nobody correcting every move. So it is with reluctance that she turns the task over to her successor, Sister Francesca. Of course, while we are all supposed to learn to do all the chores, none of us is eager to fight for this one. When I do mow a small section one day, I run over some rocks, making a terrible racket and worse yet, breaking the blade. My heart seizes; this is a crime requiring punishment. Since everything is held in common, any breakage, even of a glass, has to be proclaimed to the community. After confessing it privately to Sister Myra, she tells me I must kneel before the crucifix in the dining room at dinnertime and proclaim, "Reverend Mother and dear sisters, I wish to confess that I broke the blade on the lawnmower." I flush and bend my head to hide my embarrassment. This is the first but I'm sure not the last time I will have to make such a public confession.

Even these occasions are not without amusement. Once Sister Lily broke a phonograph record at afternoon recreation. That night, rushing back late from an errand, she slid down on her knees as dinner began, confessing: "Reverend Mother and Dear Sisters, I wish to confess that I broke a record!" Whose, I wonder? Roger Bannister's four-minute mile? A muffled giggle rippled across the room.

So I spend more time in the laundry or in the coif-making

room than outdoors. This job has some things in common with mangling sheets. We feed the snowy linens into a pleating machine, the air pungent with steaming starch, then remove them carefully and form the coifs on flat pieces of tin, cover with another tin, then press them with old flatirons until they dry and hold their shape. There is no uniformity in these; they have to be formed according to very picky individual specifications. When you have little control over your wardrobe, you apparently become more particular about what you can control. Plus, I reflect more than once, many sisters feel it is their job to help the Lord try the new sisters in their resolve to work without complaint. Although one of us might mutter under her breath as we work, we rarely erupt in the outbursts of anger or frustration that would have felt so good. Instead we suffer up our little trials in silence, as Sister Myra taught us.

It is fun to be wearing our habits, even though they are very hot – a little like a costume in a play. We enjoy practising the proper way to slip our thumb and first two fingers under the pleat of the habit and to lift it, along with the covering scapular, as we climb stairs. As I climb, the songs from the "Sound of Music" run through my head. The musical opened on Broadway in 1959 and its songs were often played on the radio and TV when I was at home. Sometimes I imagine that I am the mischievous Maria, whose lover – someone new, of course, not Barry – might whisk me away to cherish me as Maria had been cherished. Part of me still wants romance. I find it's best not to think about that part of my life anymore. Most of the time, I am content with my new way of life. When we are working, the scapulars, originally designed as aprons, ironically come off. We put on our other aprons, a splash of bright colour over the black and white. If we are scrubbing or doing something equally heavy duty, we pin up the floor-length habits to the waist. Then our pretty little pastel petticoats are displayed, another little splash of vanity. I wonder if I will ever be free of that flaw.

A couple of weeks after reception, God decides to test my ability to bear pain gracefully. All that heavy work in the heat and maybe just a little punishment for my vanity has led to a large boil festering under one of my arms. Sister Myra sends me to my dear nurse, Sister Freda.

"Oh, you kids, you will wear deodorant and clog up your pores. Now look what you've done to yourself," she chides. "All right, you're going to have to wear a poultice of bread and milk for a few days till it opens."

"Can't I just have a doctor lance it?" I plead.

"Oh, no, that's a waste of money. Here, sit down in the little room off the kitchen and I'll come and warm some milk for you. The poultice will draw out the infection. I'll bring some bandages."

When Sister Freda applies the poultice of bread soaked in warm milk to my arm, it actually feels soothing, though the milk dripping down my side into my undershirt doesn't feel pleasant. I'm going to stink like sour milk in this heat.

"Now you know how to do it and you can do it yourself or get one of the other novices to help you. Apply it three or four times a day.

So for the next four days, my classmates help me through this ritual. The boil grows and looks uglier and uglier – grey and yellow with points of white. The pain becomes excruciating. In bed, as I try to fall asleep, I weep into my pillow and pray for release. How I'd love to take a sterile needle and prick it but I'm sure Sister Freda would yell at me. So I toss and turn all night long.

On the fifth morning, though, I wake from a deep sleep. The towel I've been using to keep the sheets from dripping milk is wet with a pile of thick pus. It is disgusting but Lord, do I ever feel better. It must have burst in the night and my body relaxed and got some much-needed sleep. I go to the bathroom to clean it up.

When the alarm goes, I peek into Sister Faith's cell and proudly raise my arm. She gags and covers her mouth but then does a quiet clap to celebrate my release. After breakfast, I see Sister Freda for a minute to tell her the good news and she is not surprised. As she bandages my wound with antiseptic and clean gauze, she says, "See, I told you bread and milk would do the trick. You just had to have faith that God would relieve your suffering in His own good time."

So I thank God but also pray that will be my last boil ever. When I tell Sister Myra she says, "Put on your good habit for today. We'll wash that other one. Frankly, Sister, you're smelling like a sick baby." Humiliating but true. I'm glad to wash all that infection down the drain. Now I have to decide whether to use deodorant and risk another boil or to smell sweaty all the time. I think of girls in high school gym classes who were the butt of cruel jokes because they reeked of perspiration. Even now I'm not ready to be like one of them. I risk the deodorant.

Chapter XII

A True Calling

Everyone's favourite charge is the sacristy. The altar linens are crisply starched, the vestments of rich colours trimmed in gold. Our sacristy is a tiny storage alcove by a small toilet near the side door. Father enters this way. It is nearly always washed with sunlight and smelling of incense. The sacristan's job is to make sure everything that Father needs to wear is carefully laid out. We have to learn the names of these articles so Sister Myra instructs us one day.

"First, this rectangular piece of cloth called the amice goes on the priest's shoulders and is tied around the neck; then this large loose white vestment is the alb." She demonstrates on Sister Monique, making her the priest, causing us to giggle. "Next, he ties the alb with a long rope known as the cincture. Around the neck goes this sort of scarf called the stole, the same colour as the main vestment, the chasuble, which goes over the top. The colour changes according to the season or feast. So there is green throughout the long Pentecostal season, for instance, or violet for Advent and Lent."

I struggle to memorize all this. Amice, alb, cincture, stole, chasuble – I photograph them in my mind to quiz myself later.

"The communion paten or metal plate must be in its

burse. See this little purse-like object. The colour of the burse matches the chasuble. Next, the polished chalice is properly placed on the altar, along with the book containing the complete ritual of the Mass with all its prayers and readings."

At last we're dealing with something that so obviously connects to my calling. I find it much more appealing than laundry or lawn-mowing. I've done my share of manual labour at home but this is new and actually fun.

The sacristan lights the beeswax candles before the Mass and extinguishes them afterwards. Such a fine little feeling of power accompanies this task. The cleanup doesn't take long, so it is an easy, high profile position. It also has its singular benefits: after Mass on Friday, the sacristan has to drink whatever wine is left over – unconsecrated, of course – and then to wash the cruets. I love this job and begin to develop a taste for white sauterne wine. It's a lot better than the Mogen David I'd sampled at Christmas dinners at home.

Our attempts at meditating are strengthened by spending more time at it. Because we don't get out in the world as often as the other members of the community, we are able to focus on our interior lives better. After all, we are brides of Christ. We want to spend as much time alone with our Bridegroom as possible – like brides on their honeymoon.

In my hearts of hearts, I know that I still have a lot of rough edges to sand off. So whenever we are free from the obligations of work or study, I head to chapel where I read a little something to inspire me from the Bible or other spiritual books. Then I stop to ponder the great mysteries of God and His universe. The quietness is a boon to a girl like me from a large, noisy family. Sometimes I feel that I am able to rise above my interest in the world and connect more closely with The Beloved Christ. More and more I feel the religious life is my true calling.

The aspirants, our closest friends, especially Megan and Bonnie in my case, have gone home for the summer. We won't be seeing our families until Christmas, so it is natural for us to become attached to the old novices and to Sister Myra, who is both a loving mother and a tough taskmaster. She has high standards in everything, including our language. As taskmaster she tries to convince us that criticizing one another's mistakes in grammar and syntax is actually a gift of charity. To me it feels like continuous carping and gets on my nerves. It does make keeping silence easier though. In that, at least, we can't make a mistake.

"Su - *per* - flu - ous, sisters, with the accent on the second syllable. Not su - per - *flu* - ous, as most people say." Sister Myra takes delight in our makeover. I guess this part of our education isn't superfluous then?

When we may talk, we share our misgivings and our occasional feelings of making progress on the long hard road to holiness. "Do you get this meditation thing?" Sister Monique asks one morning during our coffee break. Shaking her head she adds, "I find it so hard to concentrate on one passage. I keep slipping away to past memories."

"It's hard, I agree," I say snatching a chocolate square left over from yesterday. "We're so used to letting our thoughts wander all over the place. It takes a lot of self-discipline."

Sister Faith suggests, "I've found if I like the book I'm reading, or if the saint's actions really inspire me, I can concentrate quite well."

"When you're not nodding off," Sister Francesca teases. Faith's natural ease at napping anywhere is becoming a favourite joke among the novices and obviously the old Paula still lives in Sister Francesca, because she still delights in picking on Sherry/Faith.

A little spark of anger lights up Sister Faith's eyes. "What about you? I see your eyes closed and your head back often enough when you're supposedly contemplating some mystery. Who knows whether you're awake?"

"At least she isn't snoring," Monique jokes. We chuckle.

Our frail human bodies sometimes let us down and we can count on our colleagues to notice.

We regularly attend classes in which we study the Holy Rule of St. Benedict. St. Benedict was the founder of monasticism and we are proud to be his followers. We learn the historical observations of our community, as well as the modern adaptations particular to St. Anselm's. Sister Myra says, "I expect you to memorize large sections of the Holy Rule, St. Benedict's guideline to perfection." Of special importance is the one on obedience which begins with "The first degree of humility is obedience without delay," which we must follow without question. She tells us, "The term obedience applies to anything that we're told to do by a superior, from the laundry to your studies to your future careers as teachers or nurses." We nod obediently.

In our classes with her, Sister Myra not only teaches us the ways of the religious life in general but also shows enough wisdom to treat us individually whenever possible. A scholarly woman herself, she encourages our exploration of the great religious books including the writings of St. Augustine and St. Benedict. Maybe she knows more about the workings of our hearts than she lets on. Or maybe, like Sister Agnes, she can read minds. At any rate, Sister Faith and I, who both entered St. Anselm's with our minds crowded with memories of our young men, are the novices she encourages to read about St. Augustine's terrible struggles with the flesh. Maybe I will get to work my way through that wonderful library after all. Following Myra's advice I read St. Augustine but no nettles for me, thanks. I'm over Barry anyway. Christ is my only lover now.

In the chapel, a little later, anxious to notify my classmates that I'm awake and meditating, I turn the page on *The Imitation of Christ* by Thomas à Kempis and try to absorb it.

~ ~ ~

On July 11, the feast of St. Benedict, Sisters Moira, Mina and Krista profess their first vows and six of the junior sisters pronounce their final vows. Because this is really the holiest community event of the year, even the novices are allowed to attend as well as any of the aspirants in the area. Both Megan and Bonnie do. I see them in the church but I can't talk to them on this day.

We dress in our Sunday habits, the ones we received on reception day, with our best coifs and starched white veils. The haircuts are now three weeks old and are starting to grow out a little, which makes them less itchy and very comfortable under the veil on a hot summer's day. We have learned to walk modestly, heads bowed, with hands under the scapular when we are not using them – very difficult for me to talk like that. Unlike some orders, we Benedictines do not wear a rosary as part of our habit but we have a slash in the habit at pocket height and many of us keep a rosary accessible in our petticoat pockets from this slash. A hanky is usually in that pocket as well. Many of the older, more devout nuns walk around the grounds, "telling" their beads, as one can guess from the way their hands move through the slash.

The new novices ride to St. Patrick's in a separate car from the rest of the community, driven by Sister Myra. Although we will be able to celebrate to a degree with the community after the ceremony, we are not to mingle with the world and our behaviour is under careful scrutiny. Sitting at some distance from the altar, I confirm that I can't see very well from a distance. I'm not yet ready to overcome my vanity and ask Sister Myra if I may consult an optometrist. Sister Freda might call it a waste of money anyway. For today, I just strain my eyes to take in the beauty of this ritual.

This ceremony is even more awe-inspiring than our reception was. The old novices pronounce their vows for three years, promoting them to the rank of junior sister. Their white veils are traded for black ones. Then the six former junior sisters promise to remain faithful until death to their vows to the Pope, the Bishop and the community of St. Benedict. They lie down on a red carpet spread at the foot of the altar. To the strains of solemn music, they are covered with a black funeral pall. While they are prostrate, a bell tolls their deaths to the world. It is impressive, beautiful, even a bit frightening. When the pall is removed, the sisters stand, their faces glowing, transformed and somehow lifted above us spectators. Mother Dorothy places a black and gold ring on their third fingers, right hand, symbolizing their permanent marriage to Christ.

A wave of sadness shatters my rapture when I realize that little chipmunk-cheeked Sister Philomena, who helped me with my trunk when I first arrived, is not among those making her vows. I must ask Sister Myra about this later.

Now the music is joyful, loud and triumphant as the newly professed sisters, led by Mother, process out of the church. "Praise to the Lord, the Almighty, the King of creation," I sing with all my heart as we, the community, follow. Once outside, the rest of the nuns line up to become a reception line. Sister Myra quickly whisks away her novices, lest we be tainted by contact with the lay guests.

We drive back to the priory, free to talk and ask questions, yet aware that today is not our day to be served but to serve. We quickly remove our scapulars, pin back our veils, put on our colourful aprons and begin helping Sister Adele organize the feast. She good-naturedly orders us about and warns us not to sample too many of the goodies. We had our big day less than a month ago. If we are able to hold fast to the course, we know that next year on July 11, we shall be celebrating again.

Although we are not allowed to mingle with the relatives of the newly professed sisters, the rest of the community ensures that we feel one with them. We're content to sneak a peek at the visitors. On this special occasion, many of our sisters have come from the various missions to share in the solemnities. Their warm overtures at friendship more than make up for our isolation from the outside world. What else do we need? We are brides of Christ and accepted members of a loving community. Life is simple and good.

At suppertime we have a pickup of leftovers and are able to sit anywhere on the grounds. I give big hugs to the new junior sisters, who are delighted to be released from the rigours of the novitiate. They will soon leave us novices behind as they move from our dorm down to the porch on the second floor. Here descent is a promotion. I hug my friend and dresser, Sister Scholastica, now a fully professed nun. I know she'll be sent off on mission at the end of the summer, so I have to take advantage of moments like these to connect with her.

"I'm so happy for you," I gush. "I can't wait to make my vows."

"It is truly a profound and wonderful experience. I'm glad you're going to be my little sister in Christ," she says, squeezing my hands.

She moves on but I overflow with affection. I've missed spending time with Sisters Freda and Agnes, to whom I've become attached and I want to take advantage of this pickup supper to chat with them, as I did in the old days. They are seated close together at one of the picnic tables.

"May I join you?" I ask.

"Of course, Sister Bridget, please do. How are you settling into life as a novice?" Sister Agnes asks.

"Oh, it's great. I'm learning so much. Of course, we're working pretty hard in the laundry and so on but I can't complain."

"It suits you, little one," Sister Freda says. "You look fine in your habit. Except, let me just tidy your veil."

"Oh, thanks, Sister. Naturally I miss the gang at Benet Hall though I've enjoyed getting to know the old novices."

"The new junior sisters, you mean," corrects Sister Agnes.

"Of course," I say, lifting a spoonful of fresh strawberries to my mouth. Plop, one of them drops on my coif – my coif that was fresh and clean this morning.

"Oh, little one, you are so sloppy. There's no point in trying to clean that off," Sister Freda says, giving it a quick swipe with her napkin. "It's too big a spot. You'd have a big dimple in your wimple," she teases with twinkling eyes. "You'll just have to change it again tomorrow."

I smother a damn, knowing the other novices will pick on me for making more work for all of us. I try to laugh it off and eat the rest of my strawberries with extreme care, though the damage is done.

The day ends with a sad revelation. Finally, I have the chance to ask Sister Myra in private, "Where was Sister Philomene? Why didn't she make her final vows?"

Sister Myra chokes back a tear as she says, "Sister Philomene decided that the religious life wasn't for her, so she returned to her home in the Dells last night." Oh sure, like Sister Suzanne. Another quitter. I shake my head, swallowing my rage and sadness. People drop out without explanation. We don't even get a chance to say goodbye. It's hard for those of us who stay. It is a startling return to the reality that some people leave even after vows. That won't happen to any of us, of course.

Chapter XIII

Of Losses and Gains

In September, some of the aspirants return but not all of them. Shirley and Ingrid are not coming back and perhaps I'll never see them again. I try not to obsess about these losses but these people have become my friends. We're not supposed to become attached to people, only to God. But a new hole opens in my human heart each time this happens; I now have a half dozen new holes in it beginning with the one made by Sister Suzanne, just since I arrived a year ago.

Seven aspirants are now postulants, or at least they are now dressed in their black uniforms. They'll officially earn that title on December 8, the feast of the Immaculate Conception, when they'll receive their medals officially welcoming them to a closer connection with the community. Megan and Bonnie are both among this group. It feels strange to be on a higher rung of the spiritual ladder than Bonnie, especially as her words made me reflect on the religious life. But I know that the road to God is a long one, and I have just begun my journey.

On October 8th the community celebrates my name day, the feast of St. Bridget. At the end of morning prayers,

Mother Dorothy announces the feasts of the community members. When we enter the dining room for breakfast, a little pile of holy cards with special prayers on them and medals honouring the saints, have been set in front of my plate. We still keep silence during that meal and at lunch but before dinner, Mother says, "Praised be Jesus Christ," and we all answer "Amen." This frees us to talk.

It's like a birthday after all. All around me, people wish me a happy name day. Each of my classmates has given me a break from one of the jobs I have to do. Sister Francesca will take my next turn at lawnmowing, Sister Faith will make some of the coifs I'm supposed to shape and Sister Monique will mangle some extra sheets. During these times, I can go read or meditate. What better gift? Moments like these make me feel so close to everyone. How I wish people like Shirley and Ingrid could be here to help me celebrate.

I run into Megan outside after dinner. She wishes me a happy name day. This little interchange is legal because of my feast, though that wouldn't have stopped Megan. She looks at me with a serious expression in her eyes. "Of course," she says, "you know the community is really celebrating my birthday, or did you forget?"

"I did forget. I've been so wrapped up in the life of a novice. Happy birthday, Megan," and I give her a warm hug.

"Yeah, well, don't forget your friends now that you've moved up in the world." Her sarcasm stings.

"Of course, I won't," and I hug her again.

~ ~ ~

Three days later, October 11, 1962, Pope John XXIII opens the Second Vatican Council. This Pope, who was only elected in 1958, is very keen to renew the Church and to move toward greater ecumenism with other religions. He is a breath of fresh air after decades of a stifling atmosphere with the Piuses who continually emphasized the superiority of Catholicism over all other religions. That certainly did not improve communication among the various beliefs.

More than 2,500 priests have gathered in Rome for this Council, the first since the late 19th century. The Pope is hoping for *aggiornamento*, the Latin word for renewal. It is a word which will become commonplace during the next four years while the Council sits. The Catholic Church will change radically as a result of this Council. We pray to the Holy Spirit that our Church leaders will be guided by wisdom.

As members of a religious order, our lives will be greatly affected by what those men in Rome decide. I sigh and pray they will make wise decisions. Decisions that will make life better for all Catholics, but especially for those of us who have committed ourselves to Christ. Often I wonder why can't women run the world? Or at least have more powerful roles in the Church. Mother certainly did a better job of running our family than Dad ever did. And Mother Dorothy does a great job here. It's time for Woman Power.

~ ~ ~

All our classes are now held either in Benet Hall or in the novitiate common room since we novices aren't allowed off campus. We focus on the finer points of the spiritual life. As the Council issues decrees, we examine them in minute detail. Music becomes more important. We study the history of the Gregorian chant, which we are beginning to perform in English.

Sister Faith and I begin to take organ lessons. I am hopeless. The organ is a much more complicated instrument than a piano with all those pedals and stops. I shake my head in frustration but Sister Cecilia smiles broadly and says, "Sister, playing the organ is a skill that will be very useful once you are sent out on mission." I begin to hope and pray I'll never actually have to play the organ in church. At least I have more sympathy for Reenie's piano playing now.

We also get to know the background of the Benedictines better, which is interesting in both historical and spiritual terms. Benedict seems like a cool guy who recognized that people are weak and do not leave their foibles outside the monastery. Yet for the love of God, they can be encouraged and inspired to rise above their human weaknesses. For example, he said, "Although we realize that wine is not a drink for monks, yet few can be convinced of this. . ." He went on to define the appropriate daily allotment of wine for his monks. These were Italian men, used to a daily intake of the fruit of the vine. We, girls from American Midwest farm communities, have only sampled beer and perhaps some wine at Christmas.

Benedict was humane. Yes, we have to give up some things but not everything. I really like his motto, which could apply to anyone, anywhere: "Moderation in all things." Except sex, of course – none of that. I'm sure there are worse things in life than dying a virgin and I just have to learn to live one day at a time. "Sufficient for the day is the evil thereof," as St. Matthew tells us in his gospel.

~ ~ ~

And so, in the natural course of events, the days fly by till it is early December. Because our outings are now confined to doctors' or dentists' appointments, even the minor celebrations take on greater value and meaning. Isn't that the idea behind monasticism, after all? So lighting the Advent candles and reading the Old Testament prophecies of the coming of Christ fills us with a rather inexplicable joy. Is it possible, that I, a worldly young woman only a few months ago, can truly be moved on a profound level by these simple activities?

On December 8, the postulants receive their medals. Now I'm part of the welcoming committee. I'm glad that Megan and Bonnie and their other classmates have embraced this life as I have. Like Sister Clementine last year, I rejoice to see the growth of the community.

Chapter XIV

Staying Home for Christmas

December flies by as usual, giving us novices little time to reflect on how different this Christmas will be from the ones in the past. But occasionally there's a little niggling reminder for me that this Christmas there will be no home visits, no huge feast with the family, no hanging out with friends at Hersey, no phone calls from Barry and most certainly, no car accidents. Instead I begin to focus, as the other sisters do, on preparing a gift for the person whose name we have drawn and are keeping secret. Each sister will receive only one gift from a member of the community. We are able to hint at useful things in a general way; then whoever has our name will try to satisfy our desires as creatively as possible.

What a mess all of us younger sisters make in the storage room where, not only are our trunks full of goodies kept but also various decorations and paper supplies are stored. There are lots of secret activities going on; excitement bubbles everywhere. Although we've been imbued with "Cleanliness is next to godliness," and other tidiness maxims, we conveniently forget that as we pull things out of boxes and leave them askew, along with trails of torn tinsel and battered bows.

It is so easy to close that old lime-green door, to pretend that someone else has left the mess.

Of far greater consequence is the fact that Sister Cecilia has chosen me to sing one of the scripture readings at Matins on Christmas Eve. I'm thrilled that she thinks I am good enough to perform this task. I often hide out in odd, solitary places, practising *The Lamentations of Jeremiah the Prophet*. I'm not a great talent but I love to sing and want my performance to be perfect.

> *In the days of yore, the lands of Naphthali and Zebulun were lightly touched, but of late, along the sea beyond the Jordan. . .*

I rehearse it every chance I get. With my true tenor voice, I probably sound more like a young monk than a struggling nun.

A wonderful, real Christmas tree is put up in the library. We novices peek at it with longing as we pass on the way to and from chapel. The junior sisters decorated it and we feel sad to have been left out. Then a massive, absolutely gorgeous tree is brought up to the community room and Sister Myra assembles her charges to tell us that decorating this one is the duty of the novices. We're thrilled. This will be the best assignment ever. I love that tree. The smell of a freshly cut fir brings memories of Christmases past. I smile as I recall my dad struggling to set the family tree upright after a few too many beers, and Mother yelling at him to let her do it.

I am stunned by the magnificence of the old-fashioned, breakable decorations. Most people have begun to move on to more durable plastic ones. Unfortunately, these precious ornaments have their flaws: they do, in fact, break. Not one but two splendid golden-pink globes fall from my clumsy fingers. Clink! Clink! They tinkle so gently it is hard to believe they'll break. But the lovely balls shatter and Sister Myra turns to me with a scowl. I cry at my carelessness and stupidity. Of course, this means another public confession of my fault before dinner tonight. However, the finished tree cheers us all up. We may be dressed in black and white ourselves but I'm sure there isn't a more brilliantly decorated tree in the whole city of Eau Claire, spun with tinsel and stars.

Faith and I are then assigned the task of trimming the main door at the side of the house. Its proximity to the driveway means that it is the one where everyone enters, rather than the front door. Having had my problems with the tree, I feel this is another area in which I can publicly mess up. We work much of one afternoon, twisting wires, tying boughs and threading thick red satin ribbons through the greenery. Our fingers and noses are well and truly frozen by the time we finish our adornment and win an approving smile from Sister Myra. Now we just have to put the finishing touches on our gifts, run through the Matins lessons once more and we will be ready for our first Christmas Eve in the convent.

After Vespers and Compline, the community files into the dining room for Christmas Eve dinner. There is no wine to accompany the meal; however it has been prepared with special care. Sister Adele has a way of making ordinary food festive The aromas of both tonight's beef stroganoff – just like home – and tomorrow's sage turkey stuffing fill the room. Since we're allowed to talk, the euphoria of the season bubbles over into enthusiastic chatter. As luck would have it, I'm sitting across from my favourite, Sister Scholastica, who is back home from La Crosse for the holidays. She is finishing her degree there and I have missed her while she was away.

"So, how are you feeling about spending Christmas in the convent, my little Sister Bridget?" she asks.

"So far, it's great. I've been so busy that I've hardly had time to miss some of the traditions from back home, or, I'm embarrassed to say, my family."

"Don't be embarrassed. We all go through that transition. We're your family now," she smiles. "You'll see your birth family soon and have a lovely reunion, but just wait. Tonight and tomorrow will convince you that the convent is the loveliest place to spend Christmas."

As it turns out, she is right. Following the cleanup after the meal, the sisters go to their separate hiding places to fetch their gifts for the ones whose names they have drawn. We all bring them into the community room and place them under the dazzling tree, now the main source of light in the room. Chairs line the perimeter of the room in a surprisingly formal arrangement, so that everyone can see the other sisters' gifts.

Sister John, a rotund and jolly young academic studying nursing in St. Paul, is also home for the holidays. She plays Santa, handing out the gifts. She wears a red Santa jacket and belt over her habit and a Santa hat hangs drunkenly from her veil and band. For a second, I see a flash of my dad in full St. Nick regalia. Of course, Sister John is cold sober but no less merry than Dad was.

Once everyone is seated, Mother leads us in prayer reminding us of the true meaning of Christmas, "Let us remember those less fortunate than we are. Lord, please accept our gratitude for the bounty in this room and especially for the wonders of the friendships formed in community life." Then she solemnly pronounces the phrase unlocking our tongues: "Praised be Jesus Christ" and we answer "Amen" with forced seriousness. At once the rowdy conversations that were started in the dining room erupt and the fun begins.

The gifts are exceptional. No doubt the fact that each sister receives only one present greatly adds to its value. People have exercised amazing creativity designing gifts to please their recipients. Sister Mina bought a red plaid sewing box with leather straps for Sister Faith. It is charming. Inside are all sorts of treats, black and white thread – very useful – needles, darning egg, a home-crocheted handkerchief and some fine chocolates. I admire her gift and hope mine will be as gratifying.

I've noticed a large black doll seated under the tree. It is one of the most charming gifts in view. While I am busy examining Sister Faith's sewing box, Sister John picks up the doll and brings it to me. My mouth falls open and then spreads into a huge smile. The best gift is mine. The doll has a black face and body. On her head is a new day cap to be worn under the coif; on her arms, new sleevelets; on her feet are homemade slippers made of facecloths. She is nearly half my size but very lightweight. I had asked for new stockings. They make up the main part of her body. I swear I'll never be able to take her apart to wear them – she's too adorable. She is wearing a small serving apron that will fit me and in the pocket are all sorts of Christmas candies. I hug her and wipe away tears of pleasure. Funny, I never wanted dolls as a girl, but like Nellie in the song, who thought they were folly, preferred storybooks. Now, though, I value all the effort that went into her construction. With due respect to gifts of the past, I think this may be the best I ever received.

All the nuns laugh and clap at my delight. Sister Adele is the clever lady who created this wonder. Not only is she amazing in the kitchen but she obviously knows her way around a sewing machine. "Well," she says, as I thank her, "I thought that one of our youngsters needed a doll." Everyone bursts into peals of laughter.

Once the other gifts, herbal teas, special soaps, small books for meditation, have been passed out, we toast the season with unspiked eggnog and cookies. By now it is ten o'clock. Many of the older sisters will remain visiting in the community room until it is time for midnight Mass. Sister Myra leads the novices upstairs for a little rest. I rise again in less than an hour greeted by the smile of my new doll sitting on my chair. We dress carefully in our best habits and head down to the chapel for one of the major celebrations of the Church year.

First, we sing the Christmas Matins. The retelling of the prophecies of old which predicted the coming of Christ brings our focus away from the materialism which we've just been enjoying, back to the centre of our lives, our bridegroom. To my relief, I do a commendable job of singing my prophecy. It feels wonderful to participate so fully in this solemn celebration. This is followed by the midnight Mass, an explosion of song and ringing bells to celebrate the birth of Christ.

After Mass, we gather in the dining room for more food, though I am almost too tired and excited to eat. There certainly will be no sleep for me tonight. Some people don't go to bed at all. It is the one night of the year when the celebrations never stop.

Christmas day is marked by more wonderful rituals, more fabulous food. The aromas of turkey and all the trimmings waft through the house, triggering memories of home. I choke back a big lump of sadness as I think of my family. We receive more visits from the sisters from our missions in the city, St. Patrick's and Regis. We play games – charades and cards – and go for a long walk. Finally, we eat a magnificent turkey dinner. By early evening, like the spiritual youngsters that we are, we novices can barely keep our eyes open. I know I am not the only one who is glad when Sister Myra suggests that an early night might be a good idea.

"Well, Sisters, what did you think of your first Christmas in the convent?" she asks as we reach the third floor common room.

I speak first, "It was beautifully simple and simply beautiful."

The others nod – for once, in wholehearted agreement.

I reach my bed and there, still waiting for me is my beloved gift, my doll. Clad in gifts meant for me, she symbolizes my new life. She continues to smile at me as I close my eyes.

~ ~ ~

Although Christmas day is over, the whole wonderful season is just beginning. Two weeks without classes, lots of skating and playing in the snow. We even go sledding and tobogganing out at the property where our new Priory is going to be built. The many hills provide thrilling and occasionally, dangerous slopes. A few knee injuries result from these forays. Fortunately, nothing very serious and not to my knees.

A highlight of the holidays is a visit from our families. They come on the Sunday after Christmas. It is a fixed date, no choice for them. The fact that a terrible blizzard is underway does not stop them from coming. Maureen tells me privately that the drive has taken twice as long as it should have and that the conditions are perilous but Mother didn't want me to be disappointed. Of course, she and my siblings miss me too. I watched at the window for what seemed like hours for their arrival, excited to see them again after so long.

We are assigned to Father's dining room as the place for our visit. It is a bright room with lots of windows, so we can watch the storm outside. Since we haven't seen each other since Reception Day six months ago, we have much to talk about.

"What was your Christmas like?" Teresa asks. She leans forward, eager to hear another tale from her old roommate.

"Well, I have to admit that it was really wonderful, much better than I expected it to be." I proceed to recount my stories.

They listen with quizzical expressions. Am I trying to make it sound better than it really is so that they needn't feel sorry for me at missing a real family Christmas?

"You mean you genuinely enjoyed it? Weren't you just so lonesome?" Maureen asks.

"Not really. Of course, I missed all of you but there were forty of us here to celebrate. It was fun as well as beautiful. Look at our gorgeous decorations everywhere."

"Yes," she says with pinched lips, "the nuns seem to have plenty of money."

"Now, Maureen. . ." Mother warns her. Don't embarrass me here, her warning look suggests.

They fill me in on how the family celebrated, show me pictures of Rita's new baby Kathy and tell me what is happening in Spring Valley and the world. To my surprise, I really don't miss any of the things they are telling me about, though I'd like to see the baby. My new life is more than sufficient. Even the gifts they have brought, practical and useful – a brief case, a Bible, new slippers – funny doggy ones – are not my main interest anymore. Of course, I appreciate their thoughtfulness and feel sorry to have little to give them but all of that matters much less to me than it has in the past. Am I settling into a way of religious poverty?

After a wonderful lunch of vegetable beef soup, salad, fresh bread and plum duff, there are brief visits from Mother Dorothy, Sister Myra and others. Mom feels she had better leave soon. The snow has continued throughout the visit. She knows the roads will be a terrible challenge, so they say goodbye. In the next letter from home I learn that the family stopped at Grandma's that night, four miles from home – as far as Mom felt she could go in that blinding blizzard. I feel relief along with underlying guilt that they went through so much for me.

Once again, we know we will not be seeing each other for

six months, not until Profession Day on July 11. However, gradually I am coming to terms with this new way of life. Once I have made first vows, they will be able to visit monthly. We are all content when we say goodbye: no tears, no wavering in my commitment. I quickly get ready for Vespers and rejoin my new family.

~ ~ ~

The heavy snow has to be dealt with the next day. Since it is warm and bright, the sisters are in a merry mood as we clear the driveway and sidewalks. It has begun to melt and is very heavy so Sister Faith and I decide to approach it from opposite ends. Though we mean to be efficient, if we had thought it through, we'd have realized this plan is fraught with danger. The routine goes well at first: we each start at one end of a small section, push towards the other, one slips the edge of her shovel under the other, and we lift together. Slide, lift. Slide, lift. Near the end of the shovelling, we are feeling larky, so we speed towards each other as fast as we can with shovels full of snow. We lift together and BAM! Faith's shovel hits me square in the eye. Liquid begins to flow from my eyes. Faith, checking it out, hugs me and assures me, "Oh Bridge, I'm so sorry. At least it's not bleeding." So tears then, I guess? Well, why not? It bloody well hurts and my coif is wrecked too, buckled in the middle as the shovel raised upward. Rats! I bite back the urge to swear aloud. Sister Freda pushes her way through the crowd of nuns that is now surrounding me.

"Now what have you done, little one?" Actually, I don't think I have done anything, though I suppose I would agree that lifting our full shovels together is a foolish shortcut. "Okay, let's put some snow on this right away to keep it from swelling."

At least treatment is close at hand and I don't have to shovel any more that day.

Sister Myra takes me to the novitiate and gives me a cup of hot cocoa. She fusses over me and tells me to rest in the comfiest chair in our little community room. I hadn't done this for attention but I am starting to enjoy it.

Unfortunately, the eye still swells and more alarmingly, it turns black – actually red, blue and purple – and "Sister Fender-Bender" now becomes the butt of many new jokes. Somehow I never imagined I'd get my first black eye at the hands of another nun in the convent.

Chapter XV

Rebirth

Winter speeds by. The days roll on with work and study until Lent is nearly over. The sky is brighter both when we get up in the morning and when we are having dinner. The sisters take turns reading from lighter spiritual fare during most of the lunches and dinners. Breakfast is fairly brisk. People leave as soon as they finish, because the demands of their days vary. Weightier tomes by Kierkegaard and De Chardin are reserved for dinner when people have more time to reflect on what is being read. Sometimes I wonder how we manage to digest food and complex ideas at the same time – or if anyone does.

For the novices, laundry and coif-making continue to fill a lot of the time when we aren't praying or studying. We are skilled at these tasks now so they're less onerous. In fact, there is a lot of satisfaction in seeing the job well done.

Sacrifices during Lent as a preparation for the singular joys of Easter will climax in an attempt to fast all day on Good Friday. Also, each sister is expected to spring houseclean her "large charge" – her special housekeeping task – before Easter. These rotate. I am lucky enough to have the library and nearby sacristy at the end of Lent. For me, these are the most appealing places to be. Even taking all the books off the shelves to dust and then replacing them has its delights. I have time to get a really good look at what the library has to offer. Of course, it does mean that I have to clean all those wide windows, something I never learn to do as well as Sister Myra would like – too many streaks, not enough elbow grease. I blame the use of vinegar and newspaper instead of some more expensive window spray. The acid stings my nostrils; I am covered with newsprint. Fortunately the windows are a lot cleaner than I am.

In the sacristy, I once again empty the wine cruet on Friday and fill it with fresh wine. Of course, none of us pours that precious liquid down the drain. Even though it is acceptable and well known, we novices still giggle about drinking it because of its inherent naughtiness and we do it surreptitiously.

On Maundy Thursday, before the big fast on Good Friday, the sisters celebrate a type of Last Supper. This is one occasion on which we do have wine for dinner – not much but a glass each if we want it. After all, it's mandated in the Bible and in the Holy Rule. Along with that we have bitter herbs, such as endive and unleavened bread, usually pita. We are allowed to talk but the solemnity of the occasion keeps us from getting too frivolous. We are certainly much more reserved than we had been on Christmas Eve. Still it always feels good to chat to real people after spending so many hours trying to learn to talk to God.

Good Friday services are very long, from noon until three, to commemorate the three hours that Christ hung on the cross. The priest leads us as we relive the stations of the cross with much kneeling or standing. My back aches and hidden sweat trickles down my skin under the heavy habit. I am fasting until the services are over. At times, I fear I will once again topple from my prie-dieu in a faint. The kneeler is thinly padded so I occasionally sit back on my chair to keep upright. The many lessons and prayers drone on, without any elaborate ritual. There is still a sense of anticipation for something more when it finally ends.

I now allow myself to eat something. I am feeling pretty dizzy, yet proud that I have proven to myself that I can make this kind of sacrifice. After all, look what Christ did for us.

If Good Friday is very basic in every way, Holy Saturday is a festival of lights, incense and bells and the fragrance of the paschal candle – fresh beeswax. This is the eve of the church's greatest feast. Like most people, I always thought Christmas was a bigger deal than Easter. Now the scales have fallen from my eyes. I realize that Christ's rising from the dead to atone for our sins is in fact the high point of the liturgical calendar.

Easter dawns bright and beautiful. Outdoors the daffodils are pushing through the thawing ground; the grass has green highlights amid the brown remnants of a dry autumn and cold winter. Inside, sweet-smelling lilies deck the altar, the paschal candle stands proudly at the right of the altar and hymns of joy fill that little chapel.

> *Alleluia, alleluia, let the holy anthems rise.*
> *Let the choirs of heaven chant it to the echoes of the skies.*

My favourite Easter song and I can sing as loud as I please. Spring and ritual combine to fill us with hope.

The food served that day is exceptional: fresh pineapple chunks and wonderful pastries for breakfast, along with eggs scrambled with savoury fresh chives. There is an elegance to the presentation that I'm not used to from home. After the main meal of ham and mashed potatoes with all the trimmings at midday, families of the professed sisters begin arriving. Most of the aspirants and the postulants also have company. For everyone but the novices, there is a big Easter egg hunt on the wide grounds of the Priory. We novices are only allowed to look on at a discreet distance from the front porch, lest we mingle with worldly influences. Nevertheless we joke about who will find the eggs we have hidden so well and have our own moments of fun.

Sister Francesca giggles, "Look at Sister Freda, rushing around after eggs. Who would think she could act so silly? What a nunny-bunny!"

"Are you kidding?" interjects Faith. "She's the one who's always leading the tomfooloery. She's so mis-***chie***-vi-ous. Remember when. . ."

"***Mis***-chie-vous, Sister, only three syllables to mischievous," Sister Myra corrects her. Sister Faith blushes. Even on Easter the Pronunciation Police are on duty.

"Really?" I ask. "Everyone I know says mis-***chie***-vi-ous."

"But that doesn't make it right, Sister," Sister Myra says in her hard-to-argue-with manner.

"Oops! Sister Mina just stepped on that egg I left in the grass," Sister Monique says, putting her hand to her mouth. We all laugh. "Look at the mess on her good shoes." Sister Mina glances at the novices who must be to blame for her fate.

"That was predictable," says Faith, trying not to be the only one who looks foolish. She shrugs and looks away.

The egg hunt rolls on as we observe from a safe distance, making blow-by-blow comments.

On the following day, to commemorate our Lord's meeting with the apostles on the way to Emmaus, the sisters traditionally take a long walk. Even the novices are allowed to come along. For this occasion, we have to wear black veils. This is meant to keep the public from questioning why the cloistered nuns are "out." We walk all the way to the new Priory property again. This time, we don't have to rush back so quickly and it is much cooler than it had been in September of my Postulant year. Fortunately, there's unlikely to be a recurrence of my fainting episode. After a picnic lunch, we return home at a normal speed. We spend a lovely afternoon able to converse in our little common room, or just reading and meditating upon the mysteries of our religion.

Easter, with its themes of rebirth, confirms for me my decision to embrace the religious life. If I had any doubts as to whether I will ask to be allowed to profess my first vows in July, they are dispelled at this time. I can hardly believe that less than two years ago, I was so reluctant to embrace the religious life. There are still a few months to go; I know there will be a few little trials but at this stage, I feel confident that I want to spend my life as a sister of St. Benedict.

~ ~ ~

In late May, the community goes out to the property for a ground breaking ceremony for the new Motherhouse. A local Monsignor cuts through the muddy earth with a shovel presented by one of our lay supporters. The smell of spring is in the air – dogwood and plum blossoms festoon the countryside. Twenty-five priests, as well as most of our community, members of the City Council and friends of the community have gathered for this brief but important moment. No longer are our one hundred and forty-three acres merely a place for picnics, walks and winter fun. It will be our new home in just over a year.

We examine the model with awe – a maze of walls and courtyards, looking like a small village. The many windows will treat us to a variety of views onto our woodlands which will be saved as much as possible. Besides the convent itself, there will be an academy for girls. The design will allow for expansion in several directions when needed.

Now the community efforts to raise funds are accelerated. Already carnivals, paper drives, candy sales and school collections had been a big help. Our sisters are only paid $900 a year by their schools, the hospital or nursing home, which is barely enough for people to live on, let alone to save for a huge building project. And the postulants and aspirants pay only $100 a month for room and board until they become novices. Then the community pays for everything. For a long time Mother Dorothy had been reluctant to solicit funds but lately she began to see the wisdom of accepting gifts from the families, friends and parishes of our members. I was pleased to learn that my own parish had made a generous contribution to the building fund and was continuing to raise more money.

In the early 1960's one of the sisters concocted a food seasoning from a variety of spices. Later she made a special one for poultry. This seasoning was called Anselm's Amazing Blend and thousands of bottles were sold near and far. No visit from our families would have been complete without one of the sisters checking whether the visitors had a sufficient supply of the Blends at home.

~ ~ ~

On June 3rd, another momentous event occurs: our beloved Papa, Pope John XXIII, who convened the Second Vatican Council and who has done so much to give the Church a new lease on life, dies of stomach cancer at the age of seventy-seven. When Father announces his death at the end of Mass, we can't hide our shock and grief. Handkerchiefs are pulled from those hidden pockets. We mourn his death like a personal loss. We wait for the white smoke over the Vatican to announce the new pope.

On June 18th, Cardinal Montini is elected the new pontiff. He will be known as Pope Paul VI. It will be his task to complete the work of the Council. Already the first proclamations have been staggering. The Mass is to be celebrated in the vernacular, instead of Latin, the priest is to face the people so that the altar must be moved away from the rear wall of the apse. The congregation will be praying aloud some of those prayers once strictly delegated to the priests. What an upheaval these alterations are causing. A revolution is underway. We can't even imagine how much we will be affected.

Chapter XVI

Metamorphosis

In June, seven new novices join the community. Now Bonnie, Megan, Marsha, Betty, Shelley, Rosina and Evelyn are decked out, tonsured, redressed and welcomed into the community with new names. We old novices are excited about the month ahead when we will be involved in training the new young nuns in the tasks of the novitiate. We are allowed to attend the ceremony but not to stay for any of the celebrations at the church. Just like last year on profession day, we are busy helping Sister Adele prepare for all the guests who will be coming for lunch. A year has gone by and we are still here, still happy and soon to be released from the gentle bonds of the novitiate. In less than a month, we will be able to have a lot more contact with the world. Honestly, at this moment, I don't miss it. Life is a blissful cocoon wrapping us in the silken fibres of the Holy Rule.

The days following reception find us in the directors' roles. Now we are the wise old novices, teaching the new sisters all about mangling sheets, making coifs, running the lawn mower safely and even finishing up the sacristy wine. After a year of being the low women on the totem pole, it's empowering for us to be the knowledgeable ones. I feel satisfied and content to be part of such a large group. Now we novices can play volleyball together during any warm summer evening recreation. It's fun to be reconnected to Bonnie and Megan. Bonnie, once my mentor, looks to me for answers.

Megan blows it off with mock sarcasm: "You think you really know it all now, don't ya, Bridge? Well, I'm not fooled. I've got a white veil now too and I know for sure it doesn't make you a saint overnight!" Her auburn hair peeks out of her coif on both sides of her face. According to Bonnie, Megan would not let Sister Myra cut her hair as the others did. And Sister Myra did not force her, so her reddish-brown locks are often visible.

Once when I am cleaning the library and Megan comes in looking for a book, she starts to chat. I love Megan; she is one of my best friends but I am trying hard to be the best little nun I can be. She is an iconoclast. I say with eyes lowered and in a soft whisper, "Sister, we don't talk in the library."

"Oh yeah, we don't? Well, maybe you don't but I do, if I have something to say and at that moment, I had something to say." She sighs. "Since I don't want to talk to myself, I'll leave you to be the role model for holiness."

Her irritation stings me. "I'm not really holy and I know I'm still full of faults."

"Oh, puh-lease," she interrupts.

"You'll find that this year in the novitiate does change you. At least it certainly changed me." I walk silently away, head bowed, hands under my scapular.

As I scurry away, I realize I am joyfully anticipating making my first vows. No more qualms about turning my back on the world, on marriage and children. I feel serene about the upcoming event. I love community life. So as July 11 nears, I believe that I do have a vocation and that I can find joy and fulfillment in the service of God and His Church. Has caterpillar Karen Traynor truly morphed into butterfly Sister Bridget?

When Profession Day dawns, a brilliant but not too hot July day, I am eager to go to St. Patrick's. I have slept surprisingly well, another indication I am doing the right thing. Now we novices receive another brand new habit, still made of serge but much lighter than the one we received last year. Maybe the powers in charge think we have sweated enough. When we dress with extra care this morning, we know that it will be the last time we put on our white veils. I am a bit sad about that, especially as, in my vanity, I think they make the sisters look younger than the standard black ones do. So the old Karen hasn't completed her metamorphosis?

Sister Cecilia, who will be our new junior mistress once we profess our vows, brings our new black veils to the church. Several sisters will also be making their final vows today. There is a buzz of excitement among the nuns at the renewal of the community in which many are growing old and retiring from public service.

After a grand procession, the Mass begins and at the time of the offertory, once again suitably chosen because we are offering ourselves to God and His Church, the profession ceremonies begin. First, the bishop blesses the new black veils and hands them to Mother Dorothy. Then one by one, she and Sister Cecilia deftly put the black veil over the white veil, secretly removing the pins and whipping the white veil off from underneath like a magician with a tablecloth. The black underveil is then put into its proper spot; the main veil is lifted slightly for this action. Being the eldest in religion, mine is the first to go. This method of redressing us in public instead of in the sacristy as when we became novices, is very clever and not without some suspense. I'd watched in awe last summer. It isn't difficult to imagine the embarrassment that everyone would have felt if one veil fell before the next one was in place. Probably it would have shocked the laity more than us to see a braided coif and a band perched on top, a curious form of exposure. Fortunately, Mother Dorothy and Sister Cecilia know their jobs well and soon four new black-veiled sisters take the place of the four white-veiled novices who entered the church.

Next we lie down on the red carpet that was spread so that our new black habits don't get dusty. The sisters making final profession are covered by the funeral pall. We new junior sisters just lie there, uncovered. We are only professing our vows for the first time. When I viewed this ceremony last year, it sent shivers down my spine. Now I am one of the people pledging to turn away from the ways of the world. For a few moments I feel totally removed from the world around me. Although I hear the gentle murmur of the bishop's voice, I am lost in a reverie with my Beloved. The religious life has brought me a serenity I never imagined. I don't feel I'm giving up everything, but instead gaining a special relationship with God. I feel privileged. The church bells peal, long and loud, breaking through my daydream.

At length, we all arise and the junior sisters stand to one side. Now the bishop places on the third finger of the right hand of each of the finally-professed sisters a type of wedding ring. It is gold with a black setting with the letters IHS inscribed on it. *IESUS HOMINUS SALVATORE* – Jesus, Saviour of mankind – an outward sign of their commitment to Christ.

When the Mass ends, we all process out again. Our families and friends are there and once the church has cleared, they are able to hug us and congratulate us. I fall into my mother's arms and cling tightly, while my siblings struggle to get a piece of me to embrace. No words are necessary; I feel flooded with love, of all kinds.

Today we celebrate with everyone, we visit with each others' families again, we talk to all our sisters who have come from afar. Faith's father can't resist whispering, "Well, look at

Sister Fender-Bender" as I pass. I laugh and give him a hug. Now, though we have turned our backs on the world, ironically we are free to connect with it again.

As this day ends and I kneel in the chapel thanking God for all that He has given me, I firmly believe that I have made a choice I will never regret. I plan to remain a Bride of Christ forever.

Chapter XVII

A Plethora of Changes

Life as a junior sister is very different from the novitiate. We can talk to so many more people so much more frequently. We're not hidden away from the public that sometimes comes to call. We even get opportunities to drive people to appointments in Eau Claire and beyond. Much as I enjoy these perks, especially driving, I long for that earlier simple way of life. I found it easier to strive for perfection without all the distractions of the outside.

One day shortly after profession I visit the optometrist and am fitted for glasses to deal with my myopia. They're the granny glasses that most of the nuns wear, but the hippies in the world are wearing them too, so I convince myself I'm in fashion. I put them aside when I don't need to see something distant – a trace of vanity remains.

For the most part, our lives are wrapped up with the four other junior sisters, three of them the former novices who taught us the tricks of the trade and Sister Cecilia, our junior mistress. She holds weekly classes with us to reveal more about community life and the liturgy. Since she is also the music director and sub-prioress, she's a busy lady. She has a gentler manner than Sister Myra did but of course, poor Myra was sanding rougher wood. Now we're almost perfect.

We enjoy times in the community room with the older sisters who live at the Motherhouse, putting jigsaw puzzles together, playing Scrabble and other games, discussing all manner of things. We are allowed to read the paper daily and to watch news programs on television. How worldly we seem compared to last year.

On November 22, 1963, we are shocked along with the rest of the country and the world to learn of the shooting of our beloved President Kennedy. The first Catholic president to lead the United States, he is a hero to the sisters and to me personally. I had campaigned for him, worn a boater hat with his picture on it to high school, written to him twice, asking to name school clubs after him. I had two letters with his signature. He was very real to me.

At lunchtime, as one of the waiters, I am bringing some food to the kitchen when Sister Freda, whispers to me in the little butler's pantry: "President Kennedy's been shot!"

"No! What happened? Is he going to be all right?"

"There was just a news bulletin; I heard it in the car coming back from an appointment. He's in critical condition in the hospital."

How I finish serving that meal, I don't know. Sister Freda tells Mother and she announces it and gives us permission to speak, yet our shock makes us nearly silent. A little later, Mother updates the news with word of his death.

After clearing the lunch, we hurry to the community room to watch the events as they unfold on television. The rest of life almost comes to a halt for a few days until the nation has grieved and watched little John John salute his father's casket. Even as people committed to the will of God, we find it difficult to make sense of this horrible event. Wrapped in our sorrows, we trudge from Benet Hall to classes and back to the community room in a dreamlike state to watch as much as possible on TV. We actually witness Lee Harvey Oswald being shot. It doesn't make matters better; we are all grieving and confused. It's such a personal loss and brings back memories of my father's death four years ago. I empathize with Jackie and her children and wonder how my own mother and siblings are taking the news, Democrats all at this time in their lives.

~ ~ ~

Eventually, we take up our tasks again and bury our sorrow in our work. In addition to continuing my studies at the Priory, I am very interested in the building of the new Motherhouse, as are all the sisters. Now the buildings are progressing quickly and we are slated to move into the new priory in early August of 1964. So our walks and rides frequently include a visit to check its progress, just as most people do when their home is being built. We love to figure out the placement of everything, the dorms, the dining room, the kitchen, the chapel and the girls' school, a separate but carefully integrated building. The exterior is of red Chicago bricks. Inside, the walls are dull grey poured concrete, through which a stylized wood grain has been forced. This type of architecture is very popular in monastic buildings of the Sixties.

When school ends in June, our focus becomes the task of packing for the big move. One potential deal to sell the old priory to the university falls through. Finally we have a firm offer. A wealthy young family will move in at the end of August. But we'll do our moving at the beginning of that month. We take a summer school course or two, but, otherwise, we're busy preparing for the change in our home.

Several of us have back, foot, or neck problems, so we don't have to actually lift any of the heavy boxes as they are loaded to go to the new priory. Bonnie and I are among these.

People call us the 4F Crew, after those lucky young men who were rejected for service in Vietnam because of some disability. We have a lot of laughs as we do the packing, under the supervision of Sister Adele. We wrap the dishes and kitchen utensils in loads of newspaper. The print rubs off and smudges our hands, arms and cheeks making us looking deceptively like hard-working sisters.

Sometimes we wonder if we will ever be able to empty the place of all the personal belongings of some forty women as well as all the china, linens, bedding and furniture. For a group of ladies abiding by vows of poverty, we have a lot of worldly goods. A parishioner who owns a brewery has generously given us a huge supply of sturdy boxes, so load after load of possessions is carried to trucks in boxes marked "WALTER'S BEER" and into one of his trucks with the same sign – an amusing paradox for women who only taste wine occasionally. Finally, the last cargo leaves 1328 Wilson Street. Mother, Sisters Cecelia, Myra and Agnes stay behind to hand over the keys to the new owner. Sister Myra gives the back porch one final thorough scrubbing, no lick and a promise for her. "If it's worth doing, it's worth doing well."

~ ~ ~

Meanwhile, at the new Priory, the workmen are still underfoot, as they will be for several more months. Imagine the odd mixture of elegant, holy virgins and coarse-talking, rough carpenters and bricklayers. Some adaptations are required on both sides but gradually, we come to have an amicable relationship.

One day I am walking through the hall on the way from the kitchen to the community room. Two workmen are in my way, trying to hang some heavy teak doors.

One of them, Dennis, is lifting his side of the door, so that his co-worker, Alf, can slide the door onto the fixed hinge.

Dennis accidentally lets the door slip and Alf yells, "What the fuck are you doing, Dennis? Shit! Damn! You dropped that three-hundred pound door on my toes!"

"Oh, sorry, it slipped," Dennis apologizes. He is surprised to see me coming their way. "Oh, sorry, Sister, he – I – we slipped."

"It's all right, fellas, I understand. I won't tell anyone," I say, reddening but smiling, as I walk through the pile of sawdust they have just created. "By the way, Alf, is your foot all right? Do you want me to get some ice for it?"

"Nah, I'll be okay but thanks for asking. As long as this idiot don't drop any more doors on it." Dennis grins sheepishly.

We have to vacuum and dust every day after they leave at 4:30 – cleanliness is next to godliness, after all. Still, it is fun to note the progress they make day after day. The workmen, won over by Sister Adele's baking and excellent coffee, grow to feel at home with their unlikely companions.

The long cloisters are much more typically monastic than the family-style home in town had been. Granted, the design is very modern, combining brick interior with poured cement in a rustic manner. I love to walk out the doors of the cloister to the large deck near the community room. The breezes carry fresh country smells, some of them less than pleasant, reminding me of my rural childhood. Frequently, we see deer grazing there at the edge of the woods, just like on Mother's farm. It is truly an idyllic spot. Home.

The heavy teak doors provide entranceways to the chapel, the main entrance and the dining room. Tall windows on an entire wall of the chapel bathe it in light, especially marvellous on a bright day. Pleated linen drapes in gunmetal grey sewn by a number of the talented seamstresses in the community provide privacy if needed and dissipate the sunlight in the heat of the summer. I love to wander around checking the view from the various openings. What a beautiful place.

Meanwhile, we junior sisters have been assigned to strip two dozen chairs that will now be stained to match the dark wood in the dining rooms and bedrooms. Our workplace is the huge garage under the kitchen which fortunately is wide open on these shimmering August days to keep the young sisters from destroying their brains with the fumes from the caustic chemicals. Perhaps due to our contact with the workmen, we lightheartedly call ourselves "The Strippers." We keep this nickname within the confines of the garage. Some of the senior sisters would not find this epithet amusing. It's hard work but we chatter away and time passes quickly. As least the chairs have simple, clean lines, easier than rolled legs and backs.

~ ~ ~

One day, late in the summer, Mother Dorothy calls us, one by one, into her office to present us with our obedience for the year. Of course, we are supposed to keep these private. However, they will soon be public knowledge anyway, so the first thing we do when we return to the Strippers is to report what we will be doing. For most of our group, it means staying at the Motherhouse to continue our studies. Sister Francesca and I, however, get special bonuses. In addition to attending classes here, we will be taking specialized courses at the nearby University of Eau Claire. Barry is no longer there and I don't care about him any longer anyway but I am excited that Mother Dorothy has decided I should specialize in drama. I will be taking theatre courses at the U. Sister Jeanette, who has long taught drama at Regis, wants a break and this will lead to my relieving her. This obedience feels like a gift.

Karen, aged 4. Her closed-mouth smile hides her missing teeth. This photo won a local contest and the photogapher displayed it in his window.

Karen's first communion day, aged 7 (1950), standing in front of a pine tree on the farm.

below The last complete Traynor family photo at Jim and Sandy's wedding, June 1, 1957: Back row, l. Maureen, Rita, Mother (Edith), Jim, Dad (Donald), Karen. Front, Teresa and Terry.

Karen graduates from Spring Valley High School in May, 1961 as the class valedictorian.

A sketch of Benet Hall which Karen made in art class, circa 1962.

The four brides of Christ on Reception Day, June 21, 1962: From left Karen, Reenie, Paula and Sherry (*as they were called in the book*).

Reception Day after the ceremony: Sister Bridget talks to relatives in front of Benet Hall.

Sister Bridget in the music room of the old convent during her family's Christmas visit when she was a novice (1962).

Group of junior sisters on Profession Day

– S. Faith, S. Monique,
S. Bridget, S. Moira,
S. Mina, S. Francesca,
S. Cecilia
(*as they were called in the book*)

Sister Bridget visiting with family on Profession Day.

Sister Bridget goes modern, removing the coif and band. Circa 1965.

PAX

Dear Sister Bridget,

Your obedience for the year is attending College of St. Benedict, St. Joseph, Minnesota.

May the Holy Spirit guide you in all your actions.

Sincerely in St. Bede,

Mother M. Lioness, OSB

Right A prie-dieu (*individual kneeler*)

The New Mother House

The Traynor farmhouse with some fresh paint and a deck.

The old St. Mary's Orphanage and School, Altoona

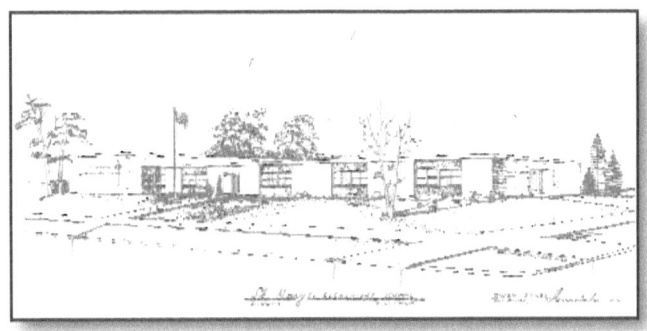

Architectural sketch of new St. Mary's School, Altoona

Chapter XVIII

Temptations

In September I begin taking four courses each semester at the U – two English classes – American and English literature – and two drama – a course in dramatic literature and a theatre production course. In the latter, I must become involved in productions, quite a change from my cloistered world of two years ago. The theatre department is a small one, so most of the people in one course are also in the other. Since I have never taken a class at a regular university before, I struggle to get used to the way the students race in late or perhaps cut class altogether. I, of course, am perfect, always on time and always prepared. The professors love me. Part of carrying out my obedience is to do things right.

One of the young men in the group flatters me with a lot of attention even though I am in a full floor-length habit, with coif and band covering all my hair plus a fair bit of my face. Bruce Carr obviously thinks it is quite a lark to flirt with a nun. I am taken aback, though I find it more appealing than I should. Below my band, my cheeks often redden when he teases me. For him, it is probably a mild bit of dalliance. For me, it is an indication that at least one member of the male species finds me attractive. We joke a lot. He is forever making scandalous comments that leave me dissolved in giggles.

"Bridget, Bridget, let your hair down." He leans to me and whispers, "Skip a class now and then. Let's go for coffee instead of sitting through this boring lecture of Gleason's." I don't take him up on his suggestions. He probably would be shocked if I did. As I discover to be typical among theatre people, his language often sounds like Alf or Dennis or someone from the farm.

"Shit, I forgot my fuckin' pen," Bruce says as he slides into his seat a few minutes after the lecture has begun. He reeks of cigarette smoke, no doubt the cause of his lateness. I find it pleasant. Reminds me of Dad, I guess. He runs a hand through his long, floppy blond hair. "Got a pen I can borrow, Bridgie?" What a nerve. This guy treats me like a normal co-ed, which I'm not, am I? "Oops, I mean, please may I borrow a pen, Sister?" That's better, Bruce.

Each year the production class must mount a show. Our group produces *Till Eulenspiegel*, a children's musical that Bruce is directing. He's in his third year of the program and is quite a talent. He chooses me to be his stage manager. I have always been the director or in my high school days, the lady on centre stage. Now my newly cultivated humility, coupled with my sense of inadequacy in the theatre arts, make me glad to take a back seat. But within a week I find that SM is an important role. Not only do I have to keep track of everyone and record all Bruce's directions but I also have to try to calm him down at times so rehearsals can proceed. During the technical rehearsal, he is a nervous wreck.

"Goddamn, lights, where the fuck is the red spot down right? That's critical to the mood of this scene."

"Actually, Bruce," I point out, "you told them yesterday that you didn't want the light up until Till starts singing 'Topsy, Turvy, Till.'"

"Okay, okay, sorry, lights, I did say that but now I've changed my mind. Bring the spot up as he's running downstage, got it?"

"Got it," the lights lady Shannon responds, sighing.

"Bridge, get that change down in the book, right?"

"Already there, boss."

"Damn, you're efficient," he shakes his head smiling and shoves his hair out of his eyes. I find myself wishing I could do that for him.

Gulp, did something just stir in my heart? I struggle to keep from giving him a little hug, or at least grabbing his hand. I breathe deeply and remain coolly chaste. I'd better avoid him as much as possible after the production finishes.

The play is finally performed on Friday and Saturday afternoons in late November. Our hard work results in standing ovations and I'm sad to see it end. I realize I love the work of production and wonder how this new passion will impact on my religious life. Being with these dramatic types fulfills me. I am changing again. Although I go home to the secure rituals of the convent, I find it hard to forget the excitement aroused by my new contacts and activities. It's so enjoyable to wander around the campus freely, sometimes to run into another old classmate from high school, to read secular books. At times, I ponder how committed I am to my life as a nun. I made first vows a little over a year ago and here I am, wavering in my stability. If I could find a hair shirt, I'd put it on.

~ ~ ~

Still, for the most part I love my life in the community. This Wisconsin winter is typical, with lots of snow and bitter cold.

At the Priory, it is all so extravagantly beautiful, set against the stark buildings that undulate around the property with the wings jutting out in a variety of directions. Long walks in the woods are a good way to unwind after a week of studying. Toboggans fly down the hills providing thrilling exercise.

Often, between prayers and dinner, I like to climb onto the flat roof and survey it all. One evening in January I bundle up against a bitter cold and watch the sun go down. The sky is magnificent, painted with crimson, fuschia, lavender, gold. The peace and quiet wrap around me like a comforting shawl. I feel very close to God at this moment. The theatre department and its cast of characters are far more than a few miles away.

~ ~ ~

Frequently, as we watch or read the national and world news, I am relieved to be in a safe part of the world. Racial riots break out across America in a long-overdue search for equal rights for blacks. I often think I should be doing more to help but Eau Claire is populated with mostly Caucasians. All we can do is pray and weep as Malcolm X is shot down leading the fight for freedom. The world is in turmoil and my own brain is very much affected by it.

The Church, too, continues its long-overdue renewal. Each autumn for four years the Second Vatican Council continued its meetings and the results are reverberating throughout Catholicism. Mass is now celebrated in English with the priest facing the congregation. Our own new chapel was designed with that in mind. We receive communion under both species, bread and wine, and we can take the host in our hands if we wish, instead of having it placed on our tongues by the priest. When he hands it to us, saying, "The Body of Christ," we answer, "Amen." Not everyone is comfortable with these changes. In some parishes, people are fighting to maintain the Latin. They feel it adds to the solemnity of the rituals. However, those of us who agree with the changes believe that we understand the liturgies better now that they are in the vernacular.

Lay people begin to play a much greater role in these services, reading lessons and helping to distribute communion. They begin to take on more catechetical duties as well. Religious communities are undergoing significant changes too. The hour of Prime has been dropped from the office. Gradually we begin to modernize our habits, which for us, means removing the band and coif and modifying the veil so that it will stay on without being pinned to anything. It sits back on the crown of our heads and comes together in the unseen back, held together by Velcro. It is lined with white and we wear either a white or black and white collar to finish the neckline of the habit. We let our hair grow; some of it shows. Megan figures she was just ahead of her time. We are allowed to return to our baptismal names, if we wish, though I stick with Bridget, not for any religious reasons, but just that I like it better than Karen. After all, I got to choose Bridget.

Some nuns begin living in small groups or couples in apartments, though of course, as a young sister, I stay at the Priory. All these alterations appear to be factors in a lot of people leaving the priesthood and religious life. We often say, "Pope John said he was opening a window. But look, it blew the priests and nuns out the door." It gives us all pause and I know that I am not the only one who spends a lot of time praying about my future and the future of the community. Where are we going? Really, what is our role in the Church? I struggle with these issues like all the nuns, but try to daily reaffirm my commitment to Christ during the many opportunities for prayer. I pray for perserverance.

Like many people in the Sixties, I am learning to play the guitar, in the hope that I'll be able to accompany religious services. No longer is the organ the only instrument allowed. Mostly I just enjoy leading the singing of what is being called a "hootenanny," singing along with a guitarist, in the community room during recreation period or on the front lawn on a Sunday afternoon. One of my favourite songs is a new one by a Canadian woman, Joni Mitchell, "Both Sides Now," a person of my own age, who is questioning life and realizing that she didn't understand it either. "*I've looked at life from both sides now/ from up and down and still somehow/ It's life's illusions I recall/ I really don't know life at all.*" I wander around singing it. Good to know that I am not alone in my confusion. Even though we have left the world, we are still affected by the political and social upheaval of the Sixties.

~ ~ ~

After that year at the university, I know that it will not be simple to remain a faithful bride of Christ. For me, practising poverty is easy – I was born into it. Obedience is sometimes a challenge but even though I am a Leo and used to calling the shots in my life, I can adapt to it. But chastity? This is going to be tough, I can see. Bruce made me aware that those chemical reactions, those exciting responses to the opposite sex that I thought were harnessed, refuse to be suppressed. I ask my Bridegroom to keep me close to Him and to help me fight temptations of the flesh.

With summer, I say goodbye to my drama classmates, knowing that I may never see them again. In some ways I feel relief but I'm torn; I'd like to continue some of these friendships. Bruce was a bad influence in some ways, but he made me laugh. His attention was flattering and he filled a role that neither the nuns nor Christ could fill. Help me, Lord, I pray. I can resist everything except temptation.

~ ~ ~

If I think I have this matter under control now, I'm mistaken. My summer obedience is teaching two weeks of catechism in Elk Mound, a nearby small town. We drive back and forth to it every day. I have been teaching there on Saturday mornings anyway, so I am at home with the parishioners, especially the children. I realize that I am pretty good at this teaching thing. It's fun. Luckily, I have enough original ideas to keep the children focused on the teachings of Christ. I mimic the firmness of Sister Gertrude and the enthusiasm of Sister Suzanne, my catechism teachers from the past. So this should be fine, a positive step on the road to Christ, right? Not exactly. The Bishop in his apparent wisdom decides to send out deacons to the parishes to help with catechetical work before they are ordained. It is very much like Mother wanting us to get a taste of teaching before we finish our degrees, or to get an idea of living at a mission before we make final vows.

Did the Bishop have to send the wittiest, the most handsome, the most intelligent and most dedicated young future priest to help us in Elk Mound? This is exactly my impression of Patrick Gregory, who is a couple of years older than I am. He is no Bruce Carr with his foul language and incessant teasing. Patrick is a man, who like me, wants to be a soldier in the army of Christ. He is as dedicated to God as I am, yet his face lights up when he sees me. In spite of my rational mind, my mortal body longs to be near him.

Once when we are playing volleyball with the children at recess, we bend down together to grab the ball. His tidy black hair is unruffled; he smells of fabric softener, nothing vile like cigarettes. Our hands accidentally touch. The warmth of his gentle hand covers mine, if only for a second. My heart races as I fight down a tingling sensation in my stomach. Two sets of laughing brown eyes meet. I take a deep breath in. We apologize. The game continues.

"Why should this be a problem?" I ask Bonnie that night. "I love God, I want to be a good sister but I feel a – a – a strong sexual attraction when I see Deacon Gregory."

"Hey, you're human, for goodness sake; don't be so hard on yourself. Making vows doesn't make the natural temptations go away. You just have to be strong. Rise above those temptations; offer them up to God. I'm sure Patrick Gregory doesn't want to lure you away from your commitment."

"Absolutely not. That's why I feel like such a fool. I wish I could just enjoy working with him without getting palpitations every time I see him."

"Oh, for cripe's sake, grow up! Concentrate on your teaching, work with him as much as is necessary but don't keep trying to find occasions to be with him, especially alone. Pretty soon you'll come to terms with your longings, believe me. "

"Okay, Bonnie, you're always right!"

And she is, though how someone who entered the convent in her Sophomore year and never had a boyfriend could have better insights on this relationship thing than I did, I never knew. Patrick and I continue to play volleyball with the kids at recess and we occasionally have to share chores in the classroom but by the end of the two weeks, I have settled down. I remind myself that Christ is the love of my life and of Patrick's. We walk away from the catechism session as good friends and nothing more.

The following June when he is ordained and then later celebrates his first Mass, he invites me to attend, along with Megan, who happens to be his cousin. I am relieved. Thank God I hadn't done anything to disturb him or to tempt him. We are united in our commitment to Christ. That doesn't mean that my wandering brain doesn't occasionally daydream about him in other ways. Once again, thanks to Bonnie, I am on the straightest course to a life with God despite its obstacles and unpredictability.

Chapter XIX

Budding Teacher

My summer school courses clue me in to Mother's plans for me for the fall, since they are Child Psychology and a course on marking – Tests and Measurements. Although I'm not quite ready to teach in a high school, I now have enough subject courses and education courses to try my hand at teaching in an elementary school. I know it's only temporary, since it was clear from my year at the U. that I'm eventually going to teach English and drama in a high school.

With summer school finished, Mother Dorothy calls me into her office in August as usual. "Sister Bridget, before you decide whether or not you want to make final vows, I want you to experience life on one of our missions. Your obedience for next year is to teach at St. Mary's in Altoona."

Her choice of school pleases me.

"Thank you, Mother. It's a nice little mission, just five sisters, isn't it?"

"Yes, Sister Jocelyn is the superior, Sister Thomas the principal and you and Sister Brenda will be the other teachers.

Sister Anna will be the cook and housekeeper. She used to work at the nursing home in Durand. I think you know some of them."

"Yes, of course, I've met them all. Sister Brenda was here as a junior sister when I arrived. I'll get to know them all quickly, I'm sure."

"As you know the school is very old but the new one is being built and should be ready in the spring."

"When do I move in?"

"Next week, if you like. You'll need to get settled in before school starts"

Next week? Excited as I am to launch my teaching career, I know I will miss life at the Priory. And I feel insecure about not measuring up as a teacher. It gives me plenty to ponder as I pull together my belongings into my trunk and two suitcases, all I now own in life. Even though I grew up in poverty, we had lots of stuff around. I feel unburdened having so little to move.

Sisters Francesca and Monique are going to southern missions, nearly a hundred miles away and Sister Faith will teach at her old elementary school, St. Patrick's, right in Eau Claire, so we'll still be able to chat on the phone and sometimes in person. It is a good setup. My final week at home is one of mixed emotions – leaving the familiar life is sad, but the new one is an adventure I look forward to.

~ ~ ~

Altoona's huge decrepit building is an ancient remnant of its past. Years ago it was an orphanage and school for boys, so there are many unused rooms. The building itself is ramshackle, unpainted and unrepaired and unfortunately, situated the length of a short train from the railroad tracks. When a train goes by, the building literally rattles; the floor creaks; old furniture rocks unsteadily. If this happens during prayers, it is hard not to giggle, especially as Sister Brenda and I would be thinking of our favourite dishwashing song:

> *The railroad comes through the middle of the house,*
> *Right smack dab through the middle of the house,*
> *Since the company bought the land.*

This internal tune mingles with the real office that we are singing:

> *I will extol Thee, my God and King*
> *and praise Thy Name for ages and forever.*

Much of the third floor is no longer in use. A smell of mildew and gathered dust pervades this area. How different from the almost antiseptic Benet Hall. No one has the time or inclination to give it that elbow grease cleaning which was a daily occurrence after the workmen left St. Anselm's. In fact, no one really cares. We all know that by spring, we will be moving into the new school that is rising on the lot behind us, a fresh-faced youngster mocking the decrepit old dowager that we now inhabit. No one is looking forward to the major decluttering that will have to take place before we make the move. Rows of old desks line one wall with broken chairs and dressers haphazardly piled on them. A faded mauve spread thrown carelessly over them only partially protects them from dust. The sagging plaster, peeling paint and the warped, unpolished floors will happily be left behind. The latter are springy and unstable.

One afternoon Sister Brenda and I go up to the third floor to see if there is anything useful for our classrooms. She is over six feet tall and uncomfortable with her height, keeping her head slightly bowed and frequently shaking it when telling one of her many funny stories. Lifting that mauve spread a little more, I confide, "Those look like rodents' nests under the desks. I've seen them at the farm."

She giggles. "I'm much more worried about falling through these rotting floorboards. I'll let you deal with the mice!"

"They might be rats. Ever think of that?"

"I hope you just have a vivid imagination," Then with a quick glance around, she decides, "There's nothing useful up here for us. Let's get out of here."

Sister Jocelyn, our superior or house boss while we are at this mission, is younger than both Sisters Thomas and Anna, probably around forty. She's uncomfortable in her role of superior, finding it difficult to arbitrate disagreements which arise. Having to keep the peace among the "brethren" isn't always as easy as it was at the Motherhouse. Here we are only five people, each with her irritating quirks. Sometimes this leads to internal strife.

Sister Anna, as short as Brenda is tall, does not relish her role as cook. She loved working at the nursing home in Durand and tells stories *ad nauseam* about her beloved patients, the friendly townspeople, and ironically, about what a great cook Sister Anthanasia was. Though she tries, her simple fare doesn't measure up to Sister Adele's. The aromas from the kitchen are rarely tempting. Sometimes the caustic odour of a scorched pot is the main welcome home from school at noon. The rest of us occasionally take turns cooking, or even, something never done at the Motherhouse, we might pick up a pizza or Kentucky Fried Chicken. Talk about going out in the world. Living so close to the tracks, we frequently have hoboes stopping by, begging for food. Sister Anna dislikes these disruptions and is stingy with her handouts but that doesn't stop the hoboes from coming. They remember her more generous predecessors, and there's an "X" marked on a tree denoting our place as a good one for food.

Our principal Sister Thomas is a stocky lady with pitted complexion. She slowly stretches out her comments. Like a commander on stormy seas, she is determined to run a tight ship.

"You know, Sister, you're the third young'un who's come here in the last six years. I get a little tired of Mother sending me the greenhorns to break in. I hope I'm not going to have to teach you how to teach."

"I hope not either, Sister. I'm as worried about my incompetence as you are. Mother must think you do a good job at teaching us young'uns, don't you think?" I smile at her, hoping she'll respond in kind. Her face remains grim.

"I suppose," she drawls. "We'll both have to get you in shape this fall."

I flash her a sheepish grin.

My task will be to teach thirty-four third and fourth graders in a rundown, crowded classroom. The chalkboards are the out-of-date black ones that are impossible to clean properly. The Zaner-Blöser version of the cursive alphabet, in both capital and lower cases, runs along the top at the front of the room. I am determined to personalize this space. Guided by Sister Brenda, I decorate that room like a Mardi Gras celebration. I hang up modern posters with poetic, idealistic messages, make little reading group seating arrangements, bring in a record player with inspirational songs, all ideas I received from my training.

Sister Jocelyn peeks in on the Friday before school starts. Her long, thin face wears a big smile. "Sister Bridget, you've done wonders here. I'm sure your students will love it."

I grin with pleasure just as Sister Brenda drops by with even more goodies, corrugated paper and tissue paper to liven it up. "Oh, yes, definitely the best room in the school," she agrees. Such support helps to keep my fears at bay, at least until Labour Day.

~ ~ ~

Finally, the day arrives – my first full-scale experience of teaching. I barely sleep a wink on Labour Day night, a not uncommon plight of young teachers, I've heard. By Tuesday morning I am bursting with nervous energy and a certain amount of terror as to what the year holds. The last sunny days of summer have given way to a chilly rain, which even after it stops, leaves the atmosphere sodden. There is a foggy mist as we walk back from Mass to start our day of teaching. Talk about pathetic fallacy – if ever the weather echoed the dreariness in women's hearts, it is today.

Eventually the kids arrive and slowly my classroom fills. Soon thirty-four shining faces – actually a few are a bit suspect – are sitting and listening as I lay out the rules and the plans for our year together. I try to follow the advice of the older sisters about not smiling before Christmas but I can't. I like the kids. They look so sweet and innocent – Diane Bridges with her pretty blonde curls and blue eyes, Julie Flohr, an eager-to-please bright brunette, freckle-faced Tommy Poldar and Kevin Cerutti, who seem to be just waiting to discover my weak spots.

It doesn't take long.

There is too much to do all at once with two classes in the room. I have to keep the Grade Fours busy while I teach the Grade Threes and vice versa. At the same time, I have to keep an eye on all of them to ensure that no one is involved in any shenanigans. I'm busier than a one-armed paperhanger, as Dad used to say.

My first dreadful day at St. Mary's reminds me of the first day of school for Scout's brand new teacher, Miss Caroline in *To Kill a Mockingbird*. Miss Caroline means well but isn't tough enough to handle the likes of Burrell Ewell. Just like me. Only the names were changed.

"Tommy, Kevin, Doug, get back to work. And put the eraser back on the chalk tray, Richard. Now you boys are going to have to spend ten minutes with me after school to make up for the time you've wasted."

"But, Sister, my dad picks me up. I have an appointment, so he'll make me come with him," whines Doug.

"I can't stay either, Sister," Kevin adds. "My mom expects me to bring my little sister home from school and . ."

"Enough," I shout, raising my voice far too much for such a minor infraction. "I'll discuss this with you boys at the beginning of lunch. And if anyone else. . . "

"But, Sister," Tommy says, "I have to walk home for lunch. I won't. . ."

"Silence. Get back to work."

It's only 9:30 and I am exhausted, yet by some combination of skill and divine intervention, I actually manage to get a couple of lessons taught. Occasionally, out of the corner of my eye, I spy my little Rat Pack exchanging glances as if to say that they have figured out how to upset me.

When lunchtime rolls around, the last thing I want to do is to keep troublemakers in, so I keep my warning brief: "You boys must not disturb the class. I'm going to let you all off this time, since it's the first day of school. I will be lenient just this once. However, you need to help me, not make things more difficult for me." I punctuate the key words as if they had hearing problems.

Richard looks up with a sad, sympathetic smile. "I'm sorry, Sister Bridget. I'll be good from now on."

"Me too!" the others agree in unison and rush off.

There, you see, I tell myself as I climb the stairs to the convent for lunch, you can catch more flies with honey than. . .

"How did it go?" the sisters all ask me as I enter.

"Oh, well, not too bad. I had some trouble keeping order."

"Now, Sister, " Sister Thomas says, firmly, "I don't care if you don't teach them a thing, as long as you hold them down. Don't be too friendly with them. I told you not to smile before Christmas."

My stomach clenches. Her edict goes against everything that I've been taught. Despite my lack of appetite I take some food and sit down. What I really want to do is to go back to bed and never return to face the little beggars. Then I cross myself and apologize to the Lord for thinking of His children as little beggars.

Too quickly, the lunch hour draws to a close. I pull myself together and return to my classroom.

If I imagined the afternoon would be better, I was wrong. After a bit of sugar at lunch, even my promising star pupils become noisy and disruptive while I work with the other group. Rather than waste more time settling them down, I just keep yelling, "Please be quiet!" Silly old me, I was so intent on teaching them something. I should have listened to Sister Thomas.

By the end of the day, I don't think I'll be able either to "Hold them down" or "teach them a thing." I barely have the energy left to climb the stairs to the convent.

Sitting in chapel I ponder my fate. I always wanted to be a teacher. I so admired Ken Ames and Bill Collins, my high school English teachers as well as Herr Lange and Herr Goldmann, my German teachers. Their classes were lively, entertaining but they still taught us a lot. We loved them. Maybe this wasn't really an appropriate line of work for me after all. Maybe I should have been a nurse, where, in general, the patients are too weak to disobey. How I wish Ken Ames were around to give me some pointers.

~ ~ ~

On the day of my dad's funeral, I was supposed to compete in the area forensics competitions in River Falls, Maureen's university town. The winners of this competition would go on to the state finals in Madison in May. Of course I couldn't miss my dad's funeral and besides, I'd been weeping for days. I could barely remember my well-memorized speech. Ken Ames coached the forensics team, often encouraging my natural ability to speak in public.

"What do you want to do about the contest?" he asked me just before leaving the funeral home where he and several other teachers had come for the visitation.

"I don't know. I guess I'll just have to miss it. I'm scheduled to speak at eleven. The funeral only starts at ten." I choked back more tears of self-pity and anger at Dad for creating this dilemma.

"There is another possibility," Mr. Ames said gently. "I could ask to have your speech moved to the latter part of the afternoon. And I could come to the church hall to get you after the lunch following the funeral."

"I hadn't thought of that. I'll ask Mom what she thinks and let you know."

When I told Mom, she said, "Of course, you should compete, if you think you'll be up to it. Your dad was always proud of your work in forensics."

And so, after the burial and the reception at the hall, Ken Ames drove me to River Falls, where I rose to the occasion and won the right to compete at State.

What a role model as a teacher. He even came out once or twice to help with the farm chores after Dad's death. "I grew up on the farm," he mused, "and I miss the work, though I know it can be drudgery when you have to do it all the time."

That was the kind of teacher I wanted to be: a helper, a guide, a friend.

~ ~ ~

As the months progress, I have some good moments. The kids seem to love the creative work that I do with them in art and music. Of course, a certain amount of chaos is attached to these classes. It's always heart-stopping to look up and see Sister Thomas, with her hands on her hefty hips, her face grimacing, saying, "Everything under control here, Sister? Because my class can hear you from way down the hall!"

"Oh sorry, Sister, yes, we're fine," I manage to say, flushing at her firm words.

Taking me aside she urges with tight white lips, "Give them a look like three days of rain!"

Right, I wonder what that looks like? Oh, yes, like Sister Thomas with her classes.

One Friday afternoon, we are creating collages with paint and coloured paper. The children are enjoying it and I hardly notice how the sound volume has risen. Tommy Poldar looks up from his creation and says to our principal who is standing rigidly in the doorway. "Oh, Sister Thomas, come and look at what I'm doing."

The sneaky little devil. He wins Sister Thomas over by his personal connection to her. His dad is on the school board and is someone she admires. She looks over Tommy's shoulder, pats it and says, "Why, Tommy, that's wonderful. Sister Bridget, that's a very good idea. You're doing some superb work with these children!"

I redden, surprised and pleased to hear my creativity being acknowledged, in front of the kids, too. They must pick up on it, for they are perfectly behaved for the rest of the afternoon. Maybe I am beginning to get the knack of this job.

That is not the end of my discipline problems, as is clear from some of the poetry I write over that first winter of teaching. After a long Christmas holiday of having fun and forgetting the responsibilities of teaching, I go back on January 5th, determined to be successful but at the end of the day, my pen explodes with this piece of doggerel:

FAILURE (OR COISES, FOILED AGAIN!)

Long vacation,
Hope restored;
Life renewed,
Grace implored.
Vigour abundant,
Plans well made;
Resolutions formed:
Then – D-DAY!

Cheery faces,
Greetings exchanged,
Scuffling, hunting,
Desks rearranged.
Pleasant beginning,
Rowdy refrain.
Noise takes over –
Foiled again!

Sister Thomas' criticism, even though justified, convinces me that I am generally a hopeless case when it comes to discipline, that even if I sometimes have success involving my students in imaginative learning situations, I am a long way from being a good teacher. I beat myself up over this, praying constantly to improve. I plan each lesson with meticulous care, hoping to win my pupils' hearts. I'm rewarded with only mixed success.

Sister Brenda tries to cheer me up over dishes. "Sister, what happened to you, happens to most new teachers. In fact it happens to most teachers, old and new, after coming back from a holiday. Everyone has had fun and no one is ready to settle down to working for six hours in uncomfortable desks in a crowded classroom."

"I guess," I say, scrubbing pots as if they at least must behave for me. "At the moment though it feels as if things will never improve."

Brenda smiles and shakes her head and bends down to whisper, "Don't let the kids and Sister Thomas defeat you."

As the winter rolls on there are some bright spots. Dianne Bridges and Julie Flohr are two of these spots of hope. They work hard and do their assignments efficiently and accurately. Sometimes, they help with the Third Graders. Adorable with curly brown hair and big green eyes, Julie is nine going on twenty-nine. She loves to help me redecorate the bulletin boards. We recite poetry together. There's a poster in the room with an anonymous poem on it that we have both memorized which we say in unison:

> *Let me laugh and dance and sing;*
> *Youth is such a lovely thing.*
> *Soon I will be old and stately*
> *I shall promenade sedately*
> *Down a narrow pavement street*
> *And the people that I meet*
> *Will be stiff and narrow too,*
> *Careful what they say and do.*
> *Let me laugh and dance and sing;*
> *Youth is such a lovely thing.*

I am so young, only twenty-two, certainly much closer in age – and temperament – to Julie than to Sister Thomas. No wonder I am more in tune with youth than maturity. Julie understands the new math, completely. I've studied it in university but my brain is still wrapped around the old approaches to arithmetic. I struggle trying to teach long division without reverting to the way I've always done it. We learned to perform the process by "guzzintas." That is, five guzzinta 125 25 times. But now we're supposed to tell the kids to estimate how many times five goes into 125, without thinking "5 guzzinta 12?" It's a subtle distinction. I try to explain:

"So whatever you've been told, forget it. Now, you need to estimate the dividend by the divisor. You should jot down your estimation on the left of the equation."

Kevin waves his arm, "Sister Bridget, I don't understand those big words you're using."

"Me neither," Tommy is relieved not to be the only one who is lost. Join the club, fellows. "What's an 'estanation'?"

Julie, who has grasped it all immediately, says levelly, "Sister Bridget, would you like me to explain it to them?"

I look at her with surprise and relief, "Why, yes, Julie, that's a good idea." She goes to the board and in language that speaks to them, clarifies my presentation.

"You see it all makes good sense. You guess how many times 5 fits into 125. That's what estimate means. You write it down on the left of the problem. Then you multiply it." She demonstrates on the board as she speaks. "So if you think 5 fits into 125 about 10 times, you try that. But see, when you multiply 5 times 10, it's only 50. So you know that it's more than 20 times, because that would only be double. And then you try 25. It's perfect."

Why didn't I think of that? The lights go on all across the classroom. The students begin to comprehend it and I gain a student teacher on the spot. She helps me check that people are on track. I can hardly resist hugging her in public. It is a leap of faith to employ her in this way but after all, my second grade teacher let me mark the first graders' work when I was only seven. Maybe it takes a teacher to recognize a teacher in the bud.

~ ~ ~

As spring approaches, a wonderful thing happens. The new school, whose progress we have watched with eager anticipation, is finished. We move in after Easter. The freshly painted rooms in the newly constructed building are a huge improvement over the crumbling old boys' school. The colours of the walls are bright and adding to the unified picture, the terrazzo floors containing speckles of all these hues – terra cotta, gold, aquamarine – are level and safe. There is no fear that one might fall through a third-storey floor and inadvertently end up like a character from the popular TV series of the era, "The Flying Nun." Our new school gives us all a new lease on life. That, along with my growing ability to keep order, makes for a much more pleasant final couple of months of the school year. Summer means I will be returning to the Priory for classes where I'll be with Megan and Bonnie and all of the old gang. I feel pretty upbeat at this time. Hard work and prayer brought me some success, and I'm proud of that.

We nuns also move to a new home – a small house across the street from the old orphanage school. It's a cozy little building and there are no suspicious sounds in the attic, suggesting the presence of rats in the old school. Sister Brenda and I can stand in the large, bright kitchen doing dishes in front of the big window overlooking the church and its grounds. We still sing while we work, including, for old time's sake, "The Railroad Runs Through the Middle of the House." The house is too small to include a chapel – we barely have enough rooms for all the sisters – so we sing our prayers around the dining room table. Only Brenda and I have decent singing voices, so the chants are croaky. Sister Anna has catarrh in her larynx causing her to constantly clear her throat. This drives Sister Jocelyn crazy. A recurring sound throughout prayers is Sister Anna's throat clearing followed by one of Sister Jocelyn's deep sighs. It's a little stressful for all of us. I sometimes pray simply for the office to be over.

My tiny room is truly a monastic cell – five feet by eleven. There is a little closet and a window, a bed and the smallest of dressers, plus a simple wooden chair where I can put a few everyday clothes. I don't even hang a holy picture on the wall for fear of adding to the sense of claustrophobia. My needs and possessions are few and I don't complain. It will be my private domain until the end of the school year.

Because we are on mission, we receive our obediences before the summer so we know whether to stay put, or to begin packing for another mission. Sister Brenda will be heading to La Crosse, a large mission in the southern part of the state. I'll miss our camaraderie and even more, our singing. To my delight her replacement will be none other than my beloved Megan. This news is almost too good to be true. Mission life is more relaxed than at the Motherhouse. Since this will be Megan's first year away from there, I'll have to try to set a good example, without seeming too goody-goody for Megan's taste. I'll also be an experienced teacher next year. Even if I haven't been a complete success, with which Sister Thomas would certainly agree, I feel more at home in the job than Megan does. Moving up always feels good. I'm looking forward to the summer and the fall.

Chapter XX

Final Vows

The arrival of summer means that I have to return to the Motherhouse to take a couple of courses, sociology and theology. But the main reason for spending part of the summer there is to prepare, along with my three classmates, for final vows. I've been so wrapped up in learning to be a good teacher that I haven't spent a lot of time thinking about the profundity of these promises. When I ponder this as I meditate in the parish church or while on solitary walks, I realize that I am simply taking the next natural step. At this moment, I believe that the life of a religious is right for me. It's not too difficult. I fit in. I love God and want to learn to love Him more. True, I don't like some of the pettiness I've seen among priests and nuns but their conduct isn't enough to stop me from permanently embracing the Benedictine way of life and yes, I've had some temptations against chastity but at the moment I feel I've got this under control. So while the prospect of final profession doesn't thrill me as a young bride is thrilled at the prospect of her wedding – that happened as I entered the novitiate after all – I'm not afraid of this new level of commitment.

Sister Monique still comes to all these classes, though we

know from the whispers in the cloisters she is not actually going to pronounce her vows with us. She is receiving an extension of her first vows, so she'll have another year before she must make a permanent commitment. I feel sad for her. My old friend Reenie, now Monique, who kept us laughing as novices, may not stay in the community. I try not to think too much about it. For a silly moment, I think of her piano practice and know I won't miss that. I smother a giggle.

~ ~ ~

July 11, 1966, the feast of St. Benedict, the day when several of us will pronounce our vows, two novices, their first vows and three of us, final vows. It is another beautiful summer day though rain overnight has left the steps a bit slippery as we walk through the courtyard in solemn procession to enter the chapel.

Since the community has resided at the new Priory for a mere two years, our class is only the second group of Benedictines to pronounce our renunciation of the world and to embrace perpetual poverty, chastity and obedience at home in our modern new chapel. The granite floors feel extremely hard compared to the more flexible and carpeted wooden floors of St. Patrick's. Still, when the appropriate moment comes, we three junior sisters in our brand new habits lie on the brightly polished mottled granite floor. No need for tricky veil games this time since we're already practitioners of the vows, evidenced by our black veils. This time the funeral pall is spread across us by Mother Dorothy, Sister Cecelia, Sister Agnes and Sister Myra, four of the chief teachers and inspirations to us in our religious life. The sharp peals of the chapel bells are at once joyous and frightening. A little shiver runs through me on this hot morning. Is this the right thing to do? Oh, God, I don't want to fail the state of holiness, I pray and remind myself, With you, O God, I can do all things.

Right, now try to remember that, okay, Bridge? I feel unsure of myself as I solemnly promise to practise the vows of poverty, chastity and obedience for the rest of my days. The rest of my days? It sounds like forever. But don't most young couples get the jitters at the moment of pronouncing their marriage vows? I calm down.

Now we rise from the floor as the funeral pall is rolled back. One by one, we kneel before Mother Dorothy as she places our rings of profession on our fingers. I lead, of course, since I am still the eldest in our religious class. Sisters Faith and Francesca follow.

After the final blessings, the sisters burst into strains of glorious song: "*Immortal, invisible God ever wise. . .*" Then the Bishop and his entourage lead the way out of the chapel. After Mother and Sister Cecilia, the new junior sisters and we three newly finally-professed sisters follow in a rank of honour. The rest of the nuns come next, like a giant wedding party. Lastly, all our families and friends, guests of the community today, parade out.

The celebration is a lovely one with brilliant floral bouquets on all the tables covered with snowy linens and lit by candles. My personal guest list is much shorter this time. It is a weekday; this is becoming routine. Former guests have more or less seen it before. Only Mother, Teresa and Terry are here from the family. The others are busy with work and their families. My old girlfriends are occupied with their babies. It's a little disappointing.

However, now I will have a lot more freedom to visit my family at home. My next visit is coming up in just a few weeks. There is cordiality among my reduced family and my new, larger community. I feel a little empty; there is no longer any big event to look forward to. Yet whatever questions may linger about my ability to remain a nun forever, I convince myself that my choice is right. At Matins tonight I am at peace with my God.

Chapter XXI

Meanwhile, Back on the Farm

Although President Kennedy is now dead and President Johnson is running the country, the Peace Corps begun during the Kennedy era is taking off. As the school year comes to a close, Maureen writes saying that she applied to enter the Peace Corps. I remember her early interest in the organization. There is a very intensive screening process, including a complete background check by the FBI. How ironic that Maureen has become involved in a government project, since she has always been outspokenly anti-government. She especially disagreed with the conflict in Vietnam and demonstrated against it. However, joining the Peace Corps is doing something good for humanity, not unlike my choice to enter the convent.

Maureen soon learns that she has been accepted for training and, on the basis of her choices, she will be sent to Ethiopia. Her summer is spent in Utah being prepared for her future role. There she meets Tom, a funny and loveable guy from New Hampshire. From the way she talks, he sounds like husband material; however, she isn't ready to settle down yet. She also speaks fondly of Dan, the musician who constantly serenades her with "Guantanamera" which he accompanies with the guitar. I fight a little twinge of jealousy that her lovers are real, tangible, unlike my spiritual beloved.

Near the end of the summer training period, some people are "de-selected," a term the government probably coined for the Corps. Fortunately, Maureen is not one of them, so she moves home in preparation for leaving for Addis Ababa in September. Mother wants us all to get together "one last time" before Maureen departs – just in case something happens to her over there.

On a splendid weekend in early August, the extended family gathers on the farm for a barbecue and celebration. Rita and Jim each have four children by now – the oldest, Jim's Tracie at nine and the youngest, Rita's Lisa, almost two. Jim's dog Nipper attends as does Rudy, Mother's wonder dog Dalmatian – the greatest shedder of all time. Jim and Wayne barbecue hamburgers and hot dogs. It's like old times, only better.

The farm looks very good. Mother rents the land to the neighbour, an old schoolmate of ours who studied agriculture. His crops are among the best in the county. The house has a new coat of paint, a gift to Mom from the older siblings. The porch is now a fine deck, built by Jim and Wayne. The best changes are gifts to Mother from Maureen. Before she leaves for Africa, she wants to be sure that Mother will be more comfortable. So she bought a new furnace with her teaching money. We don't check that out on a day like this. However, everyone tries out the new indoor bathroom that Maureen paid to have installed. The old pantry makes a perfect place for this new facility. It is complete with bathtub and the old drawers work fine for towels, washcloths and bathroom supplies.

New cupboards line the kitchen too. Rita and Wayne gave her their old ones when they renovated their kitchen. Sad as it is to admit, Mother is able to buy many more basics of life without Dad around to squander the money. It's still a struggle but now some of her kids can help her out. All I can do is pray for her. I find that a little hard; I'm a little envious of my siblings' contributions.

It is wonderful to spend this time with my family again. Though I am still in a habit with the simpler headdress, I take off my sleevelets and roll up my sleeves in an attempt to keep cool. Do I feel a little spark of envy at the great adventure that Maureen is about to embark on? Definitely. I long to see the world, something that our familial poverty has made impossible. I quell my desires, reminding myself that, after all, I have been chosen by God to serve Him in a very special way. I say goodbye and go back to Altoona to my own teaching, anxiously awaiting Maureen's letters so that I can experience her adventure vicariously.

Chapter XXII

And Back to St. Mary's

As a devout practitioner of the vow of poverty I have little to move into the larger room vacated by Sister Brenda – the tiny one had fitted fine. Yet, it is pleasant to have a desk here at home, a place to keep my books, or at least some of the many I am borrowing from the school library at this time. Even though I have always devoured every good book I could lay my hands on, I've never read the Laura Ingalls Wilder books. So my days leading up to the beginning of school are spent filling this gap. Being back in Spring Valley tweaked my interest in her. Laura was born a mere twenty miles south of my home, which she writes about in *On the Banks of Plum Creek*. I completely identify with her upbringing. I spend many a happy hour lying on my bed reading. My uneasiness about being from the farm fades as I read her tales showing her love for rural life. Yet I find myself envying her love story with Alonzo. This problem isn't going away.

The larger room has two beds. I suggest to Sister Jocelyn that I could easily share it with our newest member, Sister Megan, but Sister Jocelyn disagrees. Occasionally, she finds it easier to be the superior than usual and this is one of those times. She shakes her head trying to fight a grin. "I think we should let Sister Megan settle in a bit first, let her practise a little poverty for a while. Besides, I don't want you two talking all the time in that bedroom."

I blush. Of course, that would have happened but I also feel that I could easily share my relatively huge space. Megan has never been as comfortable with cramped quarters as I am, having been the only girl in her family and the single occupant of a large bedroom. I don't argue and figure that in time, certainly by Christmas, she will come to share my space.

~ ~ ~

With a mixture of joy and trepidation I face my second year of teaching. I learned a lot from my mistakes of the past year. Yet I am going to be teaching the upper four grades English, art and music. All those lively hormones in the Seventh and Eighth Graders terrify me. I am also going to teach Megan's Second and Third Graders music while she teaches my math – it appears to be an improved timetable.

Two new jobs that will become mine are driving the car – taking the sisters where they need to go – a job I love and playing the organ in church – a task I loathe. Mainly, I don't really feel competent enough to perform for the whole congregation. However, it is my obedience and I am determined to practise until I can do an adequate job and try to enjoy it.

With the ongoing renewal in the church, new music is being introduced. This means that sometimes we need to rehearse an unfamiliar hymn before Mass begins. Since I frequently play for two Masses on Sunday, I don't go very early unless a hymn practice is scheduled before Mass. Because the convent is right next door to the church, I usually arrive just in time to play the first hymn without panting.

I am not the only organist for the parish. Much to the priest's relief, there is a layman who is an accomplished organist. Sometimes Father Jablonski compares us, always to Frank's benefit, not mine. I don't remember applying for this job – for me it is an assignment.

One particular Sunday, the congregation does not sing any new hymns at the first Mass for which I play. But apparently, Frank had been practising a new hymn, so he and Father led choir practice before the second Mass. Nobody tells me anything about it. When it comes time for the third Mass, for which I am to play, I arrive just in time as usual. Father is not amused. He seems to think I should have read his mind and come early to rehearse the new hymn that Frank introduced. So Father says at the beginning of Mass, "Please stand for the first hymn, number 152 in the parish hymnal. I wanted to introduce a new hymn at this Mass but someone was not cooperating."

What? My head shoots up and I look down at him from my lofty position in the choir. He has just publicly and unjustly humiliated me. I am furious. I'm sure I make even more mistakes than usual as I play the hymn that I actually know very well by now. If he wants everyone to know that I am the inferior organist for the parish, I will prove him right to his chagrin. I exhale. What a charitable way for a bride of Christ to behave.

I have to pray for a lot of forgiveness that morning. A priest is God's representative, I know, and he is my superior here, so I need to love him, even if I don't really like him. I'm not looking forward to my next confession since he's the confessor. Fortunately, I have already received communion at the first Mass, because I would have found it difficult to receive it from my accuser without snatching it from his hand saying, "Liar! You didn't ask me to come for choir practice!"

I never quite get over this public humiliation. Of course, I really am not very musically gifted. My mistakes upset him when I play for weddings and funerals. Why don't people find their own organists for these special occasions? I resent the fact that I am chosen to play, not because of any talent but because no one has to pay anything for my services. Frank gets a salary, as do the cleaning lady, the florist, and even Father Jablonski. I'm the only one whose efforts go unremunerated – and I think, unappreciated.

Nevertheless, Father is too insensitive to know he hurt my feelings, and when we pass each other on the sidewalk or in school, he lifts his biretta above his thick curly locks and bows in respect. I nod in return.

Despite my ongoing struggle with Father Jablonski, life is pretty good at St. Mary's. Of course, we still have the interplay of Sister Anna and Sister Jocelyn at prayers. The clearing of the throat. The sigh. The clearing of the throat. The sigh.

Having Megan in the household is like old times. We joke together often and share our views on members of our little community as well as students that we both teach. She keeps me humble. She always brings me back down to earth when I start getting too esoteric. Yet I watch her and marvel since she is a natural in the classroom. She knows instinctively how to keep order and Sister Thomas loves her for it. Of course, she might not be quite as conscientious about preparing her lessons as I am. So we help each other out whenever possible.

Once she is teaching reading to her Grade Two class when the issue of the "schwa" comes up. Having not really looked this over ahead of time, Megan isn't sure what it is, so she nips across the hall to ask me.

"What the heck is a schwa?" she asks. I look up.

I am leaning over a student, checking his work. I recite the dictionary definition: "It's a weak unstressed sound – you can hardly hear it."

"Well, then what's the point of trying to teach it?" She

wrinkles her nose and turns on her heel. When she next speaks to the class, I hear her say, "Oh forget that, it's not important. Turn to page 56 instead."

I muse that she is probably right. Do those little duffers really need to understand the schwa? Most people pronounce words correctly because of the way they've heard them, rather than because they understand their technicalities. I learn something from Megan's practicality.

When I teach art and music to the Sevens and Eights, chaos still frequently reigns. Possibly they do admire my creativity. But they can be cruel. Besides, Sister Thomas disapproves of the disorder I create in her room and frequently points it out. When I hear the approaching click, click of her heels on the terrazzo, I hold my breath and wait for the correction.

Sister Jocelyn, on the other hand, recognizes that I am making a huge effort while still getting the knack of controlling a class. My emotions are on a roller coaster most days. I over-prepare in an effort to satisfy Sister Thomas. Have I forgotten that she said last year, "I don't care if you don't teach them a thing, as long as you hold them down"? And where's my "three days of rain" look?

Chapter XXIII

Another Fender Bender

Outside of school, there are a couple of big developments. In October, Sister Jocelyn begins taking a course at the University, about four miles away, on Tuesday nights. Ordinarily, she rides with one of our parishioners enrolled in a different class at the same time. One autumn evening, Megan and I are sitting around in our pajamas gabbing and marking papers when Sister Jocelyn phones me. The Altoona fellow who usually drives her had his class cancelled, so he has gone home early. Can I please drive over and pick her up in front of the library. Of course I say I will.

"Wanna ride along with me, Megan?" I ask.

"Sure," she says, "but let's just pull our habits over our jammies, okay?"

"Good idea," I agree.

We do exactly that. We aren't wearing coifs anymore, so it is a simple matter to pull on the habit, Velcro the veil, tuck in the collar and set off. We even keep our slippers on. In Wisconsin it is illegal not to wear shoes to control the accelerator and brake but as we set out, contact with the law that evening is the last thing on my mind.

I proceed along Fairfax Avenue as usual. Then I stop at the

light and signal to make a left turn. When the light turns green I wait, perhaps a little longer than necessary, to make sure the oncoming traffic is clear. To me it feels like a reasonable length of time to safely make my turn. And I am wearing my glasses, fortunately. Obviously, the driver behind me feels that I should have turned sooner. In a moment, for the second time in my life, I hear that sickening crash and feel the impact of another car. We have been rear-ended.

The police arrive. We pull our cars over to the quieter side street. Luckily neither of us is injured very badly though our necks and backs certainly hurt. The police officer takes Megan to sit in the cruiser. I suppress a giggle as I notice her slippered feet and pajamas clearly evident below her habit as she walks. What am I laughing at? I am dressed the same way and I am standing on the street. The officer asks me most of the questions leaning against the damaged convent car, which, although it is still drivable, looks like a write-off.

Not surprisingly, the other driver is considered completely at fault. He is charged, thanks to the testimony of witnesses as well as the obvious fact that he has crashed into the rear end of my car when I was waiting to make a left turn, with signals clearly in evidence. Those well-brought up young officers never allude to our state of undress, not even to my doggy slippers. It is a chilly night to be standing around like that and it is pretty scandalous too. Still, it will give Megan and me a story to dine out on for years. Sister Fender Bender crashes again.

When we don't show up, Sister Jocelyn correctly assumes that something is seriously wrong. She takes a cab home. When we phone to tell Sister Thomas and Sister Anna why we've been delayed, Sister Jocelyn answers and commiserates.

"Are you all right to drive home?" she asks.

"I think so. The car's in terrible shape and Father Jablonski won't be very forgiving, I'm afraid."

"Don't worry about that, as long as you're both okay." She sounds just like my mother.

"We'll be fine."

I'm actually quite shaken and both Megan and I have to see a doctor for insurance purposes, so we are allowed to take the next day off. I get permission to phone my mother. Not that she can do anything. I just need the comfort of connecting with her. The sisters are all very kind to me through this ordeal. Father Jablonski probably thinks, "Someone was not co-operating" again. But the car is insured and we soon have a new one to drive.

Ironically, the accident makes me a hero in the eyes of the Grade Sevens and Eights, especially the boys. They are awed that I could have been killed. So for a few days, at least, I have their rapt attention.

~ ~ ~

Finally, I receive my first letter from Ethiopia. Mother has been sharing Maureen's letters to her, but it's exciting to receive my own slim blue airmail envelope with colourful stamps. I gingerly slice it open with a letter opener, careful not to rip any of the precious words.

Dear Sister Bridget,

Leah and I are finally getting settled into our home and school. We've had a lot of new things to get used to all at once.

First of all, Leah is a perfect roommate. We are so compatible. As you may have heard, we live in a small cottage not far from the teachers' college where we work. We've decorated with some of our own things and gradually are buying colourful baskets, etc., which give it an Ethiopian flavour.

The first night, Leah and I decided who was sleeping in which bedroom. We went to bed and all was well for about an hour. Then the hyenas that scavenge at the nearby dump began to howl. It's a sort of whoop. Very hard to ignore.

I called to Leah and she agreed that we might be better off sleeping in the same room for a while until we got used to the nightly sounds. To my surprise, I now sleep through them most of the time.

The teachers' college is great. Our students are about seventeen and up. They want to teach elementary school and English is required, so we are explaining how to be teachers and helping them to improve their English. They're so grateful – much more than my elementary kids back home were.

I love it here. So many new experiences all the time.

Well, that's the end of this letter. Running out of space and time. Let me know if your second year is going better than the first. I'm sure it will. It always does.

Much love,
Maureen

I wipe away a few tears as I read her letter. I miss her – she's so far away – but besides that, I long to have an adventure like hers. Maybe I'll get to go to South America some day. I read her letter over and over, growing more envious each time.

Chapter XXIV

A Better Job

Meanwhile, I have another job. Since Sister Jeanette wants me to get some experience teaching speech before I am sent to take her place at Regis (our only co-ed high school, so it seems inevitable), I begin to teach a public speaking class to the girls at the Academy at the Motherhouse. It only takes me fifteen or twenty minutes to get there. Avoiding the route that would have taken me through my recent accident site, I drive the rural roads, quite a pleasant outing. Also the girls, freshmen and sophomores, since this is only the second year of the school, are so much easier to handle than my own classes. I can actually have fun with them. It is here that I begin to feel that I will eventually be a good teacher. I am more at home with the older kids.

The girls are really not a great deal younger than I am, maybe seven or eight years, so we relate well. They love to talk about the fact that they need to have boys in the school. This segregation, as they call it, is "soooo unnatural." In fact, without any boys to remind them of how obnoxious some of them can be – as I discover every day – they obsess about male contact. I see the similarity to my own longings. They are always trying to get me to organize a dance for them with the boys from St Mark's. Not that I would have been allowed to do such a worldly thing. I guess with our modified habits we seem more like girls than we had while hidden under the full habit.

The other topic that keeps coming up at the end of class or wherever the girls can sneak it in is "The Beatles," a rock group from England that is setting the music world on fire. Since their appearance on the Ed Sullivan Show a while ago, John, Paul, Ringo and George are the names on the lips of every North American teenager and many others interested in music.

I'd always kept up with the popular songs, listening to them over and over on the radio as I'd worked around home. Although it isn't explicitly forbidden, we haven't done much of that in the convent. The academy girls reveal to me the wonders of the Fab Four and many other rock groups. They enjoy teaching the teacher.

"Sister Bridget, did you watch The Beatles on the Ed Sullivan show last Sunday?" Colleen asks.

"Actually, we did. We wanted to see what all the fuss was about."

"What did you think?" Becky asks, flicking her long blonde tresses out of her eyes.

"Well, they need haircuts, don't you think?"

"Oh, Sister, long hair is in. They're adorable, especially Paul."

"I love George," Colleen insisted. "He so shy; I just want to. . ."

Becky glances at her. "Keep your plans to yourself. Not in front of Sister Bridget," she laughs.

An image of Patrick Gregory with his well trimmed locks slips across my mind.

"That's okay, Colleen, I know about teenage crushes. I was eighteen when I entered the convent after all."

"Really, Sister, tell us all about it."

I don't think I want to get into this. After all, Sister Suzanne inspired and encouraged me to join the convent and look what became of her. I'm uneasy about taking responsibility for nurturing someone else's vocation. I don't think of myself as an admirable role model and have no intentions of sharing with them the stories of my past life that they'd probably love to hear.

"Sorry but I've got to run. I'll be late for prayers back in Altoona."

"Next time," Becky insists firmly.

"We'll see." No, I know I'm not going to discuss this with them.

I grab my briefcase and race for the car. This teaching is a welcome break in the week and a generally positive experience but it keeps me on the run. Someone has to cover my last class at St. Mary's twice a week so I can teach the class at St. Anselm's. Then I have to rush home to pray the Divine Office with my own little group of sisters. I could have joined in at St. Anselm's if I wanted to. The larger group of sisters and the acoustics of the spacious chapel make for a far more heavenly choir than ours. Still, would I miss out on the catarrh and the sighs? Never.

One day, after the girls have kept me especially long, discussing various shared interests, I dash home with barely enough time to stop at the washroom before prayers. I snatch my books and slam the car door closed – on my left forefinger. Yeow! How it happened is a mystery. I only know that I am in excruciating pain for several hours. I don't feel like eating dinner – unusual for me. Even Sister Anna's basic fare is fine when I'm starving after a day of teaching. Not tonight. I can't do any work. Sister Jocelyn decides a little tot of brandy might do the trick but the throbbing nail with blood gushing up underneath it is not to be quieted. Finally, about four in the morning, I can't bear it anymore. I wake Megan, who now shares my room. She talks to Sister Jocelyn, who tells Megan to take me to the hospital emergency room. This time we dress properly, though I need a little help from Megan. We may be tired but we aren't stupid.

After a short wait a doctor sees me. He sterilizes a paper clip – no surgical equipment for this – and pokes a hole in the nail. The blood gushes out. After a moment of feeling faint from the shock, I begin to feel some relief. Hard to believe that such a minor injury can be so painful. Megan and I drag ourselves through the next day of teaching, barely able to keep awake.

~ ~ ~

The nuns are frequently invited to attend a special screening of a new film that might be of interest to our students. So the cinema owner gives us a chance to see, free of charge, some of the best films opening soon, hoping that we'll encourage our students to go. These Saturday morning features stir my heart, awakening my interest in films, history, travel and the wonders of sexual love. Barry and I never got past the heavy petting stage so it's an education.

Another sort of passion, Thomas More's sense of conviction in *A Man for All Seasons* moves me incredibly. I read everything about him I can get my hands on, admiring his struggle against both the Church and the Crown. My own doubt about the superiority of priests and religious niggles more than a little. Maybe due to the very human failings I see in Father Jablonski, Sister Thomas – in all of us. I thought we were supposed to be role models for the rest of the world. Many of us are not. I struggle with this issue in my prayers and meditations, not resolving anything.

When we go to see *Doctor Zhivago*, I am overwhelmed by the struggle for justice, the gorgeous but demanding landscapes and the exceptional love story. Can it ever be right for one person to love two people at the same time? Is it possible to love God and man with equal fervour? Am I back there again? It makes me wonder if I've grown at all spiritually in the past couple of years.

Lara writes Zhivago a note when she discovers they are in the same village after a long separation during the war: "I'm mad with joy." What a thrilling expression of love it seems to me. Watching Lara and Yuri in bed together stirs my own sexual longings. I find this very disturbing. Instead of searching for a hairshirt, I go to the library, borrow the book, and relive it. Meanwhile I continue to puzzle over how a fully professed Bride of Christ can still be overpowered by these strong temptations. They are not at the moment directed at any one person but more and more, I feel a desperate yearning to love someone like that.

~ ~ ~

One positive distraction from my inappropriate desires is beginning work on a major fundraiser for the Motherhouse. Sister Jeanette and a music teacher from La Crosse, Sister Petra, organize a musical production called *Happy Sounds* involving a large number of community members. The idea is to mount a show, perform it a few times in Eau Claire, then take it on the road to all of our missions.

Over the Christmas holidays, many of us gather for several days at the Priory to rehearse the production. We have a great time being back together. As always, it renews my spirit to return to the Motherhouse. Sister Scholastica and Sister Brenda are part of this, Bonnie too. I have missed them.

My recent mental struggles are whisked aside in the camaraderie of my sisters from all over the community. Because I am now a drama teacher, if only part-time, I am assigned the role of MC. As much as I love the spotlight, I don't like the way I, who am supposed to be holding the whole thing together, don't actually know how all the parts fit until the opening performance. This is the way Sister Jeanette likes to work. It adds a level of freshness to the production, she says. Freshness? I very nearly need to change my undershirt after the first act of the opening performance. I sweat profusely wondering what happens next. Fortunately, I learn quickly out of necessity. By the time we take the show south of Eau Claire, leaving behind a lot of satisfied fans, I have the routine down pat. We perform many times, up and down the state, raising a substantial sum to help put a dent in the huge debt incurred by the new building. These performances keep us busy many weekends till spring.

~ ~ ~

Almost without my realizing it, teaching has become more comfortable and natural. Yes, Sister Thomas still occasionally has to warn me about the lack of order in my room but eventually, she too can see that one day, I will grow into a more than decent teacher. The school year comes to a close and the obediences arrive for the next year. I almost explode with joy when I receive mine – I will be going to St. Benedict's/ St. John's next year to complete my degree in drama and speech with an English minor. Clearly, I am going to become a high school teacher, just as I always wanted. If drama isn't quite my first choice, I do enjoy it and I am still going to have the opportunity to teach English.

I will miss living with Megan and the others at St. Mary's. Father Jablonski shakes my hand cordially and grins broadly when he bids me farewell. Of course, I figure he's glad to get rid of me and I won't miss him. However, he has taught me that we have to learn to work with all kinds of personalities – another life lesson.

Before I go off to summer school, I go home to the Motherhouse for a weeklong retreat. It is wonderful to be back in a more cloistered setting, where I can reflect on the many changes in my life in the past two years.

Here I receive the sad news that my classmate, Sister Monique, has left the convent. No chance to say goodbye. I shed a small lake of tears for one of my earliest companions in the convent. It makes me wonder about the strength of my own conviction. She's not the only one. The list is lengthening. Even Sister Petra, the musical leader of Happy Sounds, Sister Mina, who taught us to mow the lawn, Sister Krista, her classmate, who taught me to make a coif.

Each loss feels like a death.

Trying not to dwell too much on this sadness, I walk around the grounds. I am moved to write some poetry:

RETURN HOME

The moss-covered grey log lies there still
In the cluster of oaks at the brow of the hill,
A bench for the thought-filled meanderer.

Clean white birch and pungent pines
Relief the convent's stately lines.
Here unobstructed, sunset is clear.

Much is unchanged but I see Time's hand
In the highway stretching below our land
And what a hayfield this lawn has become.

Not all unpleasant has Time's work been;
The mellowing of age exists within.
The rawness ripened to beauty sublime.

Often have I longed to see
These woods which set my spirit free,
This temple, strong and truthful.

My soul, long imprisoned, is freed,
Drinking deep of beauty, finding peace.
Healing arms enfold me – I am home.

During the retreat I consider that, cut off from the temptations of the world, I am very content, at least for the time being. Maybe I should have been a contemplative nun.

Who am I kidding? I find it hard enough to keep from talking during the required times of silence. How could I have spent my life with little interaction with humans? Impossible.

~ ~ ~

A week later I set off for summer school at St. Benedict's to speed up the process of finishing my degree. It's two hundred miles northwest of St. Anselm's but we are still surrounded by Benedictines, both male and female, for St. Benedict's is the large Motherhouse of which St. Anselm's is a branch; St. John's in nearby Collegeville, is the abbey of Benedictine monks. Their stark new church has much in common with the modern design of St. Anselm's.

Yes, I will still be very connected to my monastic life. Why, then, do I feel so liberated, so freed from the constraints of it? I'm a little worried as to whether I, with my tendency to get crushes on any bright or attractive man who crosses my path, I, who am thrown into turbulence by books and films, will be mature enough to withstand the temptations of being able to make so many of my own decisions.

I can't wait to try.

Chapter XXV

Liberation

The ageing campus of St. Benedict's is a big change from the modern buildings of St. Anselm's. The Motherhouse and other convent structures are rambling red brick, looking like my unconfirmed image of England.

Our own Sister Christopher is going to be my companion and roommate this summer. She is a classmate of Sister Scholastica's and someone I don't know very well yet. She is short, stocky and very pretty in a boyish sort of way. Her grey-blue eyes are intense. She often licks her lips before speaking, which she does frequently as we ride the bus together to St. Benedict's.

Like many of the main classrooms and other college structures, the theatre department and dormitories are set some distance away from the convent complex – a healthy morning walk. Since many of the girls have gone home for the summer Sister Christopher and I share a room in one of the gleaming new dorms. Most of her classes will be in theology over at St. John's. As a result we'll only see each other in the room.

She enjoys commenting on my habit of sleeping with my feet sticking out from under the covers – my Dad slept this way – with my feet crossed and one big toe between the other.

"Okay, Bridget, your feet are in place; now I can sleep," she would tease. We share our stories of life on our different missions, commenting not too charitably about our fellow sisters and the priests who work at our schools.

Summer at St. Benedict's flies by. My course work is less memorable than the people I meet. I become friends with a lot of young sisters from other communities, mostly Benedictine, from St. Cloud or St. Paul. Sister Rachel, a little older than I, who shares a lot of interests with me, including playing guitar, is looking forward to going to Expo 67 in Montreal once summer school finishes. I hardly know where Montreal is, except that our French teacher at the Priory, Monsieur Du Villes, is from a city north of there, Trois Rivières and so is Bonnie's family. I feel my rural roots.

Hoping to seem more cosmopolitan and in vogue, I continue to learn to play the guitar so maybe I can accompany songs at Mass in a modern way. It's a lot more appealing than playing the organ, less esoteric. I pick away at "Blowing in the Wind." The "new music" is one of the side effects of the Second Vatican Council. The strait-laced Church is starting to connect a bit with the hippie movement of the time and modern music, even popular songs, has become part of the liturgy.

~ ~ ~

Returning in the fall is different from summer. Sister Christopher has gone back to her teaching job at St. Patrick's leaving me to make the journey alone. Most nuns, even those with degrees, take courses in the summer for refreshment. Now the prospect of being a fulltime student away from home is thrilling to me. As pleasant as it was to have Sister Christopher with me last summer, I'm now happy to ride the bus, able to read or watch the scenery as I choose, and not to have to make conversation.

The nuns from St. Benedict's Priory meet me and drive me to the college. Since the regular students are back now the nuns do not stay in the dorms. Instead, we are segregated and I have a room in a very old building that is serviceable but homely. Most of the other women in this building are older nuns, some retired and certainly not students. Next door, though, is Sister Rachel from Illinois, who loved Expo 67 and Montreal and Sister Anne Marie from Virginia with the most delightful Southern drawl. They'll be my new friends. The rule of silence more or less prevails – at least, it is supposed to – in the hall and on the stairs, though we have quite a bit of freedom in our rooms.

However, rules aside, once I become the props mistress for a production of *The Fantasticks* that the theatre department is mounting, I can hardly stop singing the songs. Soon I know them all by heart. It would not have been unusual to walk into that building almost any time of the day and hear me singing, as I walked up or down the creaky old stairs: "*Oh you can get the rape emphatic, You can get the rape polite. . .*" I shock the older nuns with my songs. Once a grim-faced Sister Wilhomena brushes past me and I'm caught in mid-lyric. Not, I guess, the time to introduce myself as one of The Strippers.

My classes and my classmates are very appealing. Most of all, though, I enjoy my liberation. Though life at Altoona has been less restricted than it was at the Priory, I still feel that my actions were under scrutiny all the time. That is not the case at St. Benedict's. I am able to structure my days exactly as I choose, though we visiting sisters usually attend Mass and eat breakfast with the community.

On the first Sunday, a sun-dappled late summer day, I find a comfy, shady spot under a tree and spend the entire time outside of meals and prayers reading *Tess of the d'Urbervilles*. Such an intense experience, identifying with a very human woman in conflict with her society, boggles my mind. I identify with Tess even though her struggles with her family and Alec are far different from mine. This powerful piece of literature stirs again those feelings I know I am meant to suppress. Then I think about how women are blamed and punished for the actions of men and tell myself how lucky I am to be safe in my community.

~ ~ ~

On Monday I get down to the business of my education again. Although last year was better than my first year of teaching, I've always preferred being on the other side of the desk.

My course in theatre production is paramount as I really know very little about that side of putting on a play. Except for my experience as stage manager with Bruce Carr at the University, I've always either acted or directed. Somehow, Bruce Carr seems so long ago. Though I am not a natural at building or designing sets, I work hard at these tasks because I want to succeed at my courses and I know I have so much to learn.

Sister Helena, a beautiful and talented young nun from St. Benedict's, is also in my courses. She is much more skilled at most of these jobs than I am. I find myself envying both her loveliness and her ability. Our teachers Tom Corby and Dave Falstaff clearly prefer her to me, probably because she doesn't try their patience so much. It's embarrassing that I hardly know the difference between a ratchet screwdriver and a C-clamp but I am determined to learn.

As one of the requirements of our courses, we have to spend forty hours building and painting sets during the semester. For me it is the very best kind of learning experience, as I haven't been involved in such work before. The zinging of saws, the pounding of hammers, punctuated with four-letter expletives when something goes wrong – it seems to occur quite often – are a far cry from the silence of the cloister. Though some of the students quickly apologize to me, after a while, I am accepted as one of them, in my new jeans and dark green St. Benedict's sweatshirt. Occasionally, one of those expletives enters my own reactions. Damn! Shit! They just seem to fit, especially when I've spilled some paint or pounded a nail in crookedly.

I'm having a great time working on *The Fantasticks*. Although I'm still adjusting to the language of theatre types and their impatience, I enjoy watching the rehearsals and getting to know the company. Since the cast of the play is so small, the director Dave Falstaff has a double cast for some of the parts. The two fathers are played by the same actors all the time: Josh Kelsey and Kyle Craig. They are a couple of cute Johnnys, as we like to call the fellows from St. John's. Josh is a great singer but immature in an overgrown sort of way. He is stocky with curly brown hair. Kyle is a sprightly blond from New Jersey, complete with a thick Joisey accent and is absolutely adorable. He knows how to tap dance and Dave incorporates this into his performance. Kyle is trying to teach Josh the basics as well.

Both Annie, with lashes thick with mascara, and Lisa, with shining long dark hair, the two girls who play the lead, have crushes on him. Naturally, so do I. I suppose Kyle is a couple of years younger than I am but that doesn't matter. I doubt that he ever thinks of me sexually. He teases me and speaks reverently to me. While he is waiting to go on, we sit in the audience or in the wings and chat like old friends. I think about him – a lot. What if he and I were to be Lara and Zhivago? Could I love God and man? Not in that way, not in St. Benedict's book. Twice a week, I have an early afternoon class at St. John's, so the most logical thing is to eat lunch over there. On rare occasions, I run into Kyle and our now mutual friend Fitz, with his soft Kansas twang, and we share lunch. We talk about the ways that the Church is changing and where we fit into the renewal. As his shock of dark hair falls into his eyes, Fitz tells us that he is thinking about becoming a priest. It's clear that Kyle likes being in the presence of people who are dedicated to God. When I don't see him on my regular days at St. John's, a wave of disappointment spreads through me.

What is happening to me, I ask myself during a meditation period in chapel? What about my vocation, my vows? I am having such a good time that the thought of once again being sheltered from the world is unappealing. When I go to confession, I pour out my guilty desires.

"Bless me Father, for I have sinned. It has been two weeks since my last confession."

"Yes, my child, go ahead," says the kindly old priest hidden behind the grill.

"Father, I am a nun, who has made final vows. Yet I keep finding myself drawn toward the opposite sex. I have such longings."

"Sister, this happens to all of us. Are you doing anything about them? Have you given in to your feelings of lust?" Lust is pretty harsh, Father.

"Oh, no, Father, but I do want to spend time with some particular fellows. I know that Christ is my bridegroom yet I thoroughly enjoy the company of earthly males."

"Well, Sister, that is normal. And it is not a sin. However, you must avoid trying to be alone with any man where you might be tempted to break your vow of chastity – the near occasions of sin, in other words. I don't think you should feel guilty about being friends with men. Just don't fall in love with them."

"Thank you, Father. I'll try." I don't want to get into this any deeper.

"Good. For your penance, pray a rosary. Ask our Blessed Mother to help you remain chaste. If you avoid those near occasions of sin, you should be able to remain faithful to your vows. Now go in peace and may God bless you."

What a relief. I am not the sinner I thought I was. Kyle's attraction to me is without desire, but are those sought-after lunches "the near occasions of sin"? No, I reason, I don't necessarily have to be alone with him. I just want to be with him. I treasure his friendship and pore over the wonderful Christmas card he gives me. It is a large one folded several times, decorated with modern art and filled with the words of Teilhard de Chardin, a modern philosopher who has inspired religious people from all backgrounds. Much of the language strikes me as sensuous.

> *Matter, you in whom I find both seduction and strength,*
> *You in whom I find blandishment and virility,*
> *You who can enrich and destroy,*
> *The virtue of Christ has passed into you.*
> *Let your attractions lead me forward;*
> *Let your sap be the food that nourishes me;*
> *Let your resistance give me toughness;*
> *Let your robberies and inroads give me freedom.*
> *And finally let your whole being lead me toward Godhead.*

He signs it with chaste love: "My sister Bridget, I have never seen Christ's coming so clearly as I have this Christmas. You have made His love especially real for me. I thank you for being part of me. Go in love, Kyle. P.S. Joyeux Noël."

Chaste but thought-provoking. I fondle and caress that card. I try to remember what my confessor said – I avoid being alone with Kyle but at night, his words chase each other over and over in my mind. Before I board the bus to go back to Eau Claire for Christmas, we hug and kiss publicly, as everyone else from the cast of *The Fantasticks* is doing. I need a two-week break to clear my head.

It's a relief to return to St. Anselm's to pull myself together. I don't really want to discuss Kyle with Rachel or Anne Marie in our rooms. Instead I relive those moments with him in the fall during the long bus ride back to Eau Claire. I've been in the convent six and a half years now. I'm wearing Christ's wedding ring. It is time to settle down and take my commitment seriously or to move on. I pray hard over the holidays for the strength to be faithful to my vocation.

With the return to St. Benedict's, it is difficult to stick to my resolve. The school has a four-one-four organization: four credits in four months, then one credit in one month – January – when students are encouraged to take a class in something other than their majors, then four more credits in the final semester. Since I have not had enough experience in my major, I am involved in the production of *The Good Woman of Sechuan*, the stage manager, in fact. Kyle is only going to be here till the end of January, since by then he will have earned all his credits. The whole month revolves around him. He plays a small role in the play, so I feel lucky to see a lot of him and in the midst of a crowd of friends. Safe. Legal. Nothing I have to confess.

On the Sunday before he leaves, we have a special Mass at St. John's with guitar, modern songs and buckets of tears from everyone. Annie's mascara is running down her face as we sing and weep. Even Fitz, his thick black hair falling in his eyes as always, cannot hide the tears. Fortunately, I'm not wearing any makeup that could smear and betray the depth of my grief.

After Mass, we all get together for a pizza party to finally say goodbye to him. We sing the songs from *The Fantasticks* and hug each other over and over.

Deep in December, it's nice to remember, the fires of September that made us mellow...

Kyle is the core of our group. When he leaves, the group will likely disband.

What a grim time to lose a dear friend – in truth, someone I adore – the middle of winter. My days are highlighted by visits to my mailbox to see if he has written. He does. Sometimes the letters arrive at a later time than the mail is usually distributed. Is someone censoring them, a practice now out-of-date? Or is this God's way of testing me to see how long I can wait?

I find that I don't even want to see the old crowd very much unless they have had a letter from Kyle. Fitz and I sometimes share lunch in the midst of the crowd and talk about our latest connection to Kyle. Frankly, I'd rather reread my own letters, write to Kyle, or occasionally, to write a poem which expresses my loneliness.

In the Weeks that Followed: Separation

Campus crowded but unpeopled;
Cafeteria packed but empty;
Songs sung but tuneless;
Sunshine bright but chilling;
Hours busy but hollow;
Friends cluster then scatter.
He has gone.
He made the crowd into persons;
He made the mealtimes sparkle;
He brought the music to life.
He warmed the world with his glow;
He made each day a celebration.
How can I live without him?

Back to confession, Bridget. This does not sound like a virginal bride of Christ. In fact, I've made this young man an object of my idolatry. Yet I justify it in this way: Kyle loves to hang out with nuns and priests. He is the typical outstanding layperson of the late 60's. He just loves the humanity he sees in those who are committed to a higher life. I don't think he realizes how down-to-earth my feelings are for him and I certainly don't plan to tell him.

~ ~ ~

To fill in the empty spaces in my heart, I get to know a group of graduate nuns and monks and gradually, their friendship weans me away from my focus on Kyle. Still, it isn't a return to a perfectly chaste state of mind, not by a long shot. Barnabas, an intelligent and witty monk, with a chiseled jaw and severe features, sees me as the opportunity to get free show tickets. As a theatre student, I often received freebies, so that is the beginning of the association. Barnabas flirts with me. He's not especially attractive but his braininess is appealing.

I like hanging around with this clever crowd. One of my dreams is to be an intellectual, though naturally I don't think I measure up. I hate feeling like a country hick as I recall my rural upbringing – my first eight years of education spent in a little one-room country school. I hope their cerebral discussions will rub off on me. They are all working on their master's degrees and I am merely finishing up my B.A. I haven't read as many of the great philosophers or religious thinkers as they have. However occasionally I throw in an intelligent comment and they seem favourably impressed. Barnabas gives me books to read and my very own gift copy of Hermann Hesse's *Steppenwolf*. It's a challenging read for me but I struggle to make sense of it. At least I want to be able to say how it affected me even if only to impress him.

Three of this group of scholars are young deacons: a tall, freckled redhead, Larry and short, dark John, both from Wisconsin and Stef from Minnesota, whose receding hairline makes him look older than he is. These are fun guys, very flirtatious and both of the Wisconsin guys are incredibly good-looking. Did the seminary lure the likeliest hearthrobs? I can't help but think so. Larry gives me a book called *Love and Sexuality*. He signs it: "Bridget! May our awareness of the power of love in us always draw us closer to Christ our Centre. I thank God for your truly feminine sexuality. May you grow and prosper and become what you are! And may we love. Larry." Hmmm. Is it just me or is there an undercurrent of passion here?

These are confusing times. The authors of the book, professors of my course, apparently practise a platonic style of marriage, or that is the talk around campus. They even examine such a marriage in the book. And here am I a nun, vowed to serve Christ for life, constantly attracted by men, teetering on the edge of a sexual encounter. What a hopeless practitioner of the virtue of chastity I am turning out to be.

~ ~ ~

On April 4, 1968, we are all shocked to learn of the assassination of Martin Luther King, Jr., the man who struggled so hard for equal rights for blacks. His "I Have a Dream" speech at the Lincoln Memorial in August 1963 brought him to prominence. We nuns had cheered on his efforts, and now that same pain we'd experienced only five years ago with President Kennedy's death reawakens. What is becoming of America? In my heart there blooms the urge to get out in the world and fight the cause openly. Priests like Daniel and Philip Berrigan, Midwesterners like me, were leaders in the anti-Vietnam War movement. Philip had gone to jail last year for non-violent protests, and Daniel went to Hanoi this winter to try to broker a peace agreement. But what could a mere nun do? I feel impotent and long to make a greater impact on the world. Will I have to leave the convent to do that?

~ ~ ~

The academic year comes to an end and I graduate with the other "Bennies" on a bright May day. The scents of lilacs and mock orange fill the spring air with optimism as we walk around the campus with our loved ones. After a pleasant lunch for the families, which my own mother, Mother Dorothy and Sister Myra attend, we line up on the lawn. In our black robes and red and white hoods, we are an elegant lot. With great pride, I walk up to receive my degree.

After a lot of goodbyes to friends and promises to write, especially among the grad students, we hoist my trunk and boxes in the car and head off for Wisconsin where I am able to spend a week at home with my family, a reward for a job well done. On the way back to Eau Claire the nuns drop Mother and me at the farm. I'm relieved that there is now an indoor bathroom for the nuns to use. In fact, the farm looks better and better all the time. Mom's hard work has paid off.

It's a time to reflect on where I am going with my life. As a novice, it felt so easy to turn away from the world. Now that I have been on my own again, I realize how much I value my independence, the freedom to make my own decisions. I'm sure my superiors would have frowned on some of them, if they had known. They trusted me to build on my training and to continue to fulfill my commitment to Christ and look how I behaved. My mind is in turmoil. Maybe life will be less complicated when I return to teaching. My students will finally be older kids and at last, I'll be teaching my beloved subjects of English and drama. Certainly, Mom continues to struggle financially. I don't envy her efforts to keep things together. Yet being free to do as I choose, to work where and as I like is very appealing. Does that mean leaving the convent? I have a lot to meditate upon as I wander the familiar pastures of home.

Chapter XXVI

Summer with Judy in Red Rudy

Back at St. Anselm's with diploma in hand, I try to settle down to life as a Bride of Christ. I don't expect it to be easy. Thank goodness Mother Dorothy comes up with a summer job for me, both unusual and highly motivating. She calls me into her office one morning, shortly after I return from my home visit.

"Well, Sister, of course, you know you'll be teaching drama and English at Regis in the fall."

I swallow. I knew this was coming and yet. . . "I guess I expected it. After all, that's why I got this degree, isn't it? But Sister Jeanette's shoes will be difficult to fill."

"You just have to remember that you're not trying to be Sister Jeanette. You're Sister Bridget, trying to carry out God's will as well as best you can." Her benign face and large blue eyes are full of serene confidence.

"Of course, you're right, Mother." I realize, though, that my high-flying position as one of the livelier members of St. Benedict's theatre department has evaporated and I am back at the lowest rung on the ladder. "I hope I can handle the job, since, as I'm sure you know, I didn't do very well at Altoona."

Mother's eyes twinkle as she says, "Well, there are many different ways of judging how well one does. I hear that you did a lot of imaginative things with your students and Sister Jocelyn says you were an excellent member of your little community. So I have confidence that you will do a fine job at Regis too."

I feel my colour rise. "Well, thanks, Mother; I hope I can live up to your expectations."

"Oh, I'm sure you will. Sister Faith will be there too, so you'll have a classmate who is beginning just as you are."

This is a little surprise. "That's great, Mother. We'll be able to give each other moral support. What are your plans for me this summer?"

"Well, that's one of the things I called you in to discuss. St. Anselm's has been asked to help with the Headstart Program in Chippewa Falls this summer. It's a booster program for pre-school children from disadvantaged backgrounds. A small group of social workers could use a couple of us to teach the children things like music, art, drama and sports. It will be held in an elementary school in the Falls beginning in July and will last four weeks, Monday through Friday from nine in the morning till one. You'll feed them lunch as part of the program. This program is government-funded and the subsidized lunch will be prepared by ladies from the community. You'll also have to visit each family to try to encourage them to help their children to succeed in school. It's designed for children who have not had many opportunities in their early childhoods to try to get a head start before they begin school."

"That sounds like a very worthwhile program. I'd love to do it. Will anyone be working with me?"

"Yes, Sister Judy Cavell and three social workers from the area, two men and a woman."

I smile. Judy and I get on very well. She's a couple of years older than I am and has been teaching elementary school in the southern part of the state. She sings beautifully with a confident soprano voice and is very witty, a good storyteller – my kind of person.

"This job doesn't sound like work. It sounds exciting and unique. I'm sure Sister Judy will be an excellent partner." My face beams.

"I'm glad you think so," said Mother, "because that's pretty much what she said about you."

~ ~ ~

On the morning of June 6, Sister Freda wakes up the young sisters in the dormitory with news of yet another assassination – this time President Kennedy's brother Bobby, who was running for the Democratic nomination for president. After a speech in a California hotel, he was gunned down by a name we would soon know all too well – Sirhan Sirhan. I shake my head at the grievous news. "Sister Freda, you have become the messenger of doom. I think I'll run the other way when I see you coming with tears in your eyes." We hug and pass on the word to anyone who didn't wake up with her announcement. This death numbs me. I simply can't believe it. My faith is shaken by all these deaths of people trying to make the world a better place. I wonder how God can allow it, and I pray at Mass for comprehension.

~ ~ ~

When Sister Judy and I finish teaching catechism in some small towns without Catholic schools – like my own little hometown

– she comes home to the Priory where we'll be based for the summer. We immediately put our heads together and begin brainstorming our teaching plans. We're so full of ideas we're talking a mile a minute.

One afternoon we drive to Chippewa Falls to meet the three social workers, Alan, Mike, and Elaine, with whom we will be working. The lines of responsibility are drawn up so that Judy and I will not be expected to do more social work than we have been trained for. They are all committed, concerned people and we leave the meeting feeling very confident that we will be working with devoted professionals.

The group of fifteen children we will be working with ranges in age from four to six. Troubled family lives, severe illness or other family problems have prevented some of the older ones from attending school. What a challenge it will be bringing them up to speed in a mere four weeks.

The children are a motley crew, young and innocent but with clothes and bodies that could have used more washing and mending. Even in July, there are drippy noses. Sad little undernourished waifs with dull hair look at us with both expectation and suspicion. From their records we know some of these children have had very bad experiences with adults. We are determined to give them a more positive outlook on life.

Judy and I decide to "team teach," a popular trend in education at this time. Instead of dividing the children into two rooms, we keep them all in the same room and take turns leading the activities. Judy, the better singer of the two of us, leads them in simple songs while I accompany them on the guitar. I also put my drama skills to work by having them perform uncomplicated improvisations. We both play games outside in the summer sunshine that is growing hotter every day.

We drive each day from the Priory in a car that has been

loaned to us by the social workers, an old red Ford, which we soon dub Red Rudy. The half-hour drive each way passes quickly as we lament over our poor little duffers.

The visits to the parents are eye opening. Although Judy and I had both been raised in what we thought of as rural poverty, we were rich by comparison to the families of these children. Chippewa Falls has many lovely, stately old homes but just outside the town exists a veritable slum, with shacks that are in a shocking state of disrepair. These are the places to which our children return after a few hours of enrichment. One child, Joyce, is able to speak reasonably well, though we have to listen hard to understand her both for her low volume and her inability to articulate clearly. We are amazed to discover that both her parents are deaf and dumb. What a difficult environment little Joyce has grown up in. Despite these facts, she seems loved and not abused, as are many of the children. With help, she could probably fit into society reasonably well.

It is the children of alcoholics and abusive parents who have much less chance of succeeding. Sometimes, our teacher visits go beyond the bounds of our abilities to deal with the situation although one of the social workers usually accompanies us. An unemployed father, who still manages to afford liquor, shouts at us to get off his property. His long-suffering wife, with stringy hair and faded dress, stands on the porch, talking to us about little Jake. It's clear that she was the force behind Jake's involvement in the program. Although their ramshackle home is much worse than ours was, this visit causes some unhappy flashbacks of Dad's drinking problem. The parallels are similar and painful for me.

Curiously enough, considering the backgrounds of these children, they are docile and easier to manage than the more privileged children of Altoona had been. Of course, it helps to have a teacher partner in the room and the pupil-teacher ratio is nicely low. By the end of the four weeks, I have grown very fond of these little ones and begin to think that, given more time, I might have made an elementary teacher. Just watching the way Judy deals with them gives me insights into how I might have improved. For a start, she is always walking around the room commenting on the work students are doing, answering their questions. I realize I tended to keep my distance, paying too much heed to Sister Thomas' warnings of not smiling till Christmas and holding them down.

~ ~ ~

When our summer obedience ends, I get another lucky break. In order to prepare me for teaching drama at Regis, Mother Dorothy asks me if I would like to attend the National Theatre Convention in Chicago. I will be going alone, my first visit ever to the big city, staying in the hotel where the convention is held. I take the train to the city and a cab to my hotel. I am excited and impressed that Mother has enough confidence in me to send me off alone.

When I exit the cab, I stand for a moment looking at the park across the street from the hotel. Even though I was a nun living in a small city I could not help but be aware of the political riots that had erupted there during the previous couple of weeks. Here I stood at history's doorstep. The Democratic National Convention had been held nearby and Eugene McCarthy lost a fiercely fought battle against Hubert Humphrey inside. Outside protestors of the Vietnam War fought to make sure their voices were heard. Even though a few protesters felt the blows of police clubs in the process, it all ended peacefully. Abandoned McCarthy buttons are strewn across the park. I must have one as a souvenir of these troubled times in our country, and perhaps as a symbol of my own conundrum about how best to serve.

Once I am settled into the room that I am sharing with some nuns from other communities, I go for a walk. The city is hot and busy, and the caustic odours of industrial pollution give me a headache. Yet the charm of Chicago is unquestionable. Lake Michigan is an easy walk east from the hotel. How delightful to find that pocket of natural beauty in the midst of so many stunning manmade structures – the architecture of Frank Lloyd Wright, for instance, is everywhere. I visit the Field Museum of Anthropology, gawking in wonder at the dinosaurs. I long to explore more but unfortunately, I have to get back to the hotel for the opening session of the conference.

The famous mayor of Chicago, Richard J. Daley, a man who seems to own Chicago, welcomes us. Edward Albee, one of the important guests, speaks to us about his production of *The Sandbox*, which is then performed for us. I feel tickled to be so close to such celebrities.

In our free time I don't wander very far afield but many highlights of the city, the Goodman Theatre and the art museum are close by. I visit some of the finest art displays in the world. What a thrill to walk into the Art Institute of Chicago and see the classic painting by Seurat, *Sunday Afternoon on the Island of Grande Jatte*, nearly filling one wall. Here is another wonderful opportunity, a gift from the community, yet all I do is reflect on how much I love being on my own and making my own choices. It is going to be difficult to return to the gentle bonds of community life, which feel restrictive after my year and more of liberation.

~ ~ ~

Upon returning to Eau Claire I turn my mind to becoming the number one drama teacher at Regis. With my usual lack of self-confidence I worry whether I am ready for so much responsibility. I lose sleep yet I am exhilarated at the same time. I'm more than ready to go when Mother tells Sister Faith and me to pack our bags for the move to Regis in mid-August so we'll be closer to the books and equipment that we need for preparation. Mother and Sister Jeanette have always been very good friends. Mother had been the head of the business department at Regis before she became the Prioress. Now Faith and I are the new generation taking over these roles. I'm sure their hopes for us are high but they must wonder, as we do, whether we are up to the challenge.

Chapter XXVII

The Torch is Passed

God help me! I watch my first junior English class, age sixteen and older, file into my well-decorated classroom on that first day of school. These guys are big enough to throw me right out the window with little effort, and since the window slides up from the bottom and pushes up to the upper pane and I have a first floor room, such a calamity just might happen.

Enter the cast of characters: Greg, a big Teddy bear with slicked back brown hair, at six-foot-three, finds it difficult to squeeze into any desk; Gene, with the fairest Nordic colouring, looks angelic but his blue eyes gleam with devilment under his glasses; Cathy, slim and agile with a mane of curly brown hair swings in with a "who-gives-a damn attitude"; Mary with a light brown ponytail, clings to her, seemingly attached at the hip; Candy Koehn hangs back shyly, probably from years of having to live with such a problematic name; Tom, long and gangly with a high brown crew cut, smiles and studies me as if deciding how to corner my attention; David, with dark eyes and hair, who wants to be a lawyer and is keen to improve in the arts of public speaking and composition which I will teach him; Linda, a bright, beautiful brunette, eager to please, answers all my questions, and Donna, with dyed blonde hair and tasty-looking pink lipstick. She lives across the street from the convent and thinks of the nuns as her neighbours and friends, not just her teachers. A number of extras complete the crowded class of thirty-five. One semester I will teach them public speaking and the other, composition. For a moment I wonder how this drama will play out.

What's this? They listen to me? They ask intelligent questions? Perhaps all that I recalled of high school students when I was struggling with the younger children was correct, not just wishful thinking. For a start, these older kids know their marks will be very important when applying to universities and colleges next year. Also most of them are adult enough to know that first impressions are important and that teachers, no matter how objective they try to be, are affected by behaviour. Yes, Gene and Tom sometimes tease me because they have guessed correctly that I am only six or seven years older than they are but I keep a suitable distance. Now at last I dispense with Sister Thomas's admonition, "Don't smile till after Christmas." I even ignore her warning: "Sister, I don't care if you don't teach them a thing, as long as you hold them down!" I feel very comfortable with these young people. They respect me as I believe they should; keeping order in the classroom seems easy and natural. Thanks be to God. This is the first year of the rest of my life as a teacher.

Besides my two junior English classes and two freshmen English classes, I am finally teaching drama – junior and senior classes. The arts courses are electives so the students actually chose to be there. Fortunately the seniors have already had some training from Sister Jeanette. They are a huge help to me, especially light and sound technician, Steve Dickson. Steve is a young man with a shock of red hair and thick glasses. He just turned eighteen but is old beyond his years. I could not have survived without him. He understands the lighting and sound system and runs it without much direction from me – a good thing, since I know only the rudiments of technical theatre.

One of the traditional activities of the seniors is to prepare a children's play which we will perform a few times at the school for the area children. Then we will "take it on the road," mainly to Northern Colony, a huge facility for the mentally retarded located just outside of Chippewa Falls. My work with Headstart made me feel at ease with people who are intellectually handicapped. Our university psychology class visited on a field trip, so I know what to expect from the audience. I don't, however, know how to drive a truck to move some basic scenery to the site – but Steve does. He is my knight in shining armour with a chauffeur's license. He is as determined as I am to make a success of our performance. The others can drive themselves. What a relief to have such self-reliant students; my prayers have been answered.

Our audiences love *Prince Fairyfoot*, starring Greg Brown. He clomps around in huge boots – a great visual joke for kids of all ages. At Regis, we play to packed houses of paying audiences. This covers our expenses for such essentials as royalties, makeup, costumes, props and set. At Northern Colony, the kids experience volunteering for a good cause. Only a hundred or so residents are selected to join in the fun but they love it. They are a most vocal and appreciative audience. Afterwards, the students share refreshments with the residents. It is an eye-opener for my students and from their conversations, I realise they respect me more for having the courage to take the show on the road. This is something Sister Jeanette hadn't done. Since they frequently remind me that "Sister Jeanette did this; Sister Jeanette did that," I shake my head and tell them, once and for all, in our late President Kennedy's words: "The torch has been passed to a new generation of Americans." They howl and clap.

After the final performance at Regis, the cast calls me up on stage to receive fragrant red roses. I am overwhelmed with joy and the sweet smell of success – an improvement over the pervasive dressing room odours of stale socks and underwear. At any rate, directing comes naturally to me. I'm happy to have found a niche for myself. And I can do this while I work for the Lord. My first year of teaching high school is off to a great start. Of course, I still miss my friends from St. John's, but some of them keep in close touch with letters and calls, especially Barnabas, but I am not at all unhappy in my new life. Its many rewards keep me looking forward rather than regretting the past.

Encouraged by this success, both the kids and I are eager to get on with the major production of the year. Auditions are open for students throughout the school; however the senior drama students usually win the major roles. I choose a play that I had seen at the Guthrie Theatre in Minneapolis, *The Skin of Our Teeth* by Thornton Wilder. It's appropriate because it has a large cast and some interesting possibilities for a simple set. Regis is hardly the Guthrie but I do have Steve and Sister Miriam, our art teacher at Regis, to help with the design.

One tradition at Regis had been to double-cast the largest roles. This allowed for greater student involvement. Having done this at St. Benedict's with *The Fantasticks*, I knew it could be fraught with peril. However, I do double-cast the play; everyone is happy for the moment. A red-haired wonder named Pat Brady wins the role of Mr. Antrobus with both casts since the show revolves around him. He starts growing his beard right away. Some keen students play the family animals, the woolly mammoth and the dinosaur. The lead roles are the Antrobuses and their maid Sabina. It is a parody on many old plays and frequently, in the Wilder fashion, Sabina often comes out of character to clarify something to the audience, just like the stage manager in *Our Town*.

I decide to have the cast sell the tickets, since it will not only ensure a sizable audience but will give me a way of deciding which cast should perform on the extra evening in our five-show run. Whoever sells the most wins. As showtime nears, both casts are highly competitive, and they present me with money for the tickets they've sold. Unfortunately, during performances, many seats are still empty, because the cast members simply bought the tickets themselves to be sure they got to play the extra show. The auditorium feels cavernous as we play to a very small crowd. Also, the antagonism which the competition arouses teaches me a life lesson: if you're going to double-cast, be sure you have an even number of shows.

The set is supposed to look unrealistic and slipshod and that at least is a complete success. Somehow we have rigged this wooden framework "wall" to fly across and drop into place at various times during the play. It does so, but more perilously with every performance. Finally, on the last night, it simply drops to the floor. Fortunately, one of the actors – who had been drilled with "The show must go on" – says, "Oh goodness, the house is completely falling apart" and the show limps safely to its conclusion.

The cast and crew don't mind, though, since this incident simply serves to make the final set strike go faster. Afterwards we order pizza for our celebration on the clean stage. Everyone cheers as Pat shaves his red beard. Another successful production by the Regis Drama Club.

Chapter XXVIII

A Different Community

Life in our little religious community settles into a routine, though it is very different from life at the Priory or Altoona. There are twenty-five of us here, most of us teaching at Regis. Many of these sisters have been together for twenty years or more and special or "particular" friendships have formed among a couple of pairs of nuns. The community frowns on such exclusive friendships – we must love all the sisters. But they clearly do exist – at times they seem like old married couples, looking after each other. Others, quite reclusive, don't want to have much to do with anyone.

My aim is to get to know everyone. I become friendly with Sister Bonita, our principal and also the superior here at the convent. She came from a small town near mine and we know a lot of the same people. Another new friend is Sister Joan, the round-faced cook with dark-rimmed glasses. She is a natural joker and always up for a good time. I love having a cup of tea with her after classes end and sharing tales of our day's work. Of course, Faith is my old classmate and confidante. We have a lot of private discussions, talking about our successes and failures and our views of this microcosm of the community.

One Sunday afternoon, we go for a walk, Joan, Faith and I. As we walk through the lovely treed neighbourhoods, we begin to gossip.

"Regis is really different from the Motherhouse, isn't it?" I venture.

"Oh, yeah," agrees Joan. "Well, some of these women came in with the bricks you know."

"Some of them are about as lively as bricks," Faith adds.

"I think it's the fact that until recently we've only had one high school. The elementary teachers have more options. Here, if you don't get along with someone, there's no place to hide, except your own room," I say.

"And that's where many of them spend their time outside of meals, prayers and school.

Nobody sits around the community room to chat," Faith says. "That's what I miss the most – community life. Even at little St. Patrick's we had a good time most evenings sharing the events of the day."

"Yes that was true at Altoona, too. We goofed off a lot."

"For sure, you and Megan were always crazy together," Faith observes. "A couple of funny nunny-bunnies."

"Yes but even Sister Thomas, who wasn't all that impressed with me as a teacher could be a lot of laughs in the evening. We often did our Polish takeoffs of Father Jablonski."

"She's witty, in a rough way, once you get past the Prussian General exterior," Joan adds. "We were together at La Crosse for a couple of years. That's the good thing about being a cook; you get to move around a lot."

"And you're a great cook, Joan," I say, flinging an arm around her shoulder. "Sister Anna, well. . . she could have used a few lessons." She squeezes me back.

"Oh, by the way, Bridge, are you still getting letters from Barnabas?" Faith asks.

"Oh, yeah, that's your friend from St. John's, isn't it? I see a lot of letters from him for you, when I sort the mail. Is this a particular friendship?" Joan teases.

"Not really. He seems to want to keep in touch with me more than I do with him. He really is too cerebral for me. I'm not always comfortable with the level of the topics that he talks about. I guess he stretches me. He's a fan of Nietzsche and really knows classical music. Still, I like receiving letters from a man."

"I agree," says Faith. "I hear from a guy named Mack that I met in a summer course at the University. He's a Viet war vet. Very mixed up. Right now I think I'm just helping him find his way back to normalcy after some really horrendous experiences. He was at this place called My Lai, where a lot of civilians were killed by our soldiers."

"I've heard our guys committed some atrocities there. I know we blame it on what the Viet Cong did but this war had better end soon. It's turning people into animals," I say.

"Changing the subject, what do you think about Sister Sharon? I wonder if all these rumours about her and Father Redman are true?" Joan echoes the curiosity we all have felt. Her big brown eyes are full of interest.

"Yeah, where were they last weekend? She was gone and I hear that he was too. I think her days in the community are numbered." I shake my head.

It's always sobering to consider how many priests and nuns are becoming involved with each other in this post-Vatican II world. At first they begin doing catechetical work together, then they go off somewhere, supposedly to do the work of God and not long after, we hear that one or more of them is leaving. It is a widespread phenomenon. In fact, Barnabas has mentioned that he will probably be leaving his community in June. He's a monk, not a priest. I'm sure his relationship with me is not a factor in his decision but I do wonder at times whether he is practising relating to women through his contact with me.

~ ~ ~

In addition to common prayers and meals at Regis, we have to let someone in the group know where we are but we don't have to check out with anyone in particular, such as our superior, Sister Bonita. People are becoming more and more independent, so Sister Sharon's weekend away is not the only one of its kind. Other people go off for the weekend and most of these outings are probably perfectly innocent.

My own catechetical work and my interaction with the lay people on staff make me realise that some of them do as much for others as we are doing. Yet they can go home to their families at night. I watch Mrs. Shea, widowed mother of six. Her kids are great – I've taught two of them; both have acted in my plays. She still finds time to teach catechism and to help sew altar cloths for the church. What makes our work any better? Does God really need us to practise poverty, chastity and obedience in order to serve Him well? The struggle with these questions fills many of my waking hours and keeps me from falling asleep at night.

~ ~ ~

Before Christmas, one of our lay teachers invites us to his house for a party. We enjoy snacks and a couple of drinks each. It's amazing – so normal. After two drinks, Father Collie, the pastor of Elk Mound where I taught catechism all those

Saturdays four years ago and now a colleague at Regis, pulls me aside to the sunroom attached to the main party area.

"Sister Bridget, I've been wanting to tell you something and now I feel enough courage to say. . . " This sweet dumpy little man, heavy-set, balding, wearing unattractive glasses is struggling to make some sort of revelation. What? "I've – uh – always loved you."

Oh no. I frown in amazement. This is no Patrick Gregory, irresistibly handsome, or lively, charismatic Kyle Craig. This is Father Will Collie, fifteen years my senior, whom I always liked until this point. I never imagined he had special feelings for me but I certainly don't encourage him.

"Will, let's not be ridiculous here. I'm not interested in a relationship with you or any other man." While not exactly true, he doesn't have to know that; it is the strongest argument that I can muster.

"Oh, please, Bridget," he pleads, his face contorted in constipated agony, "I thought you felt something special for me too. You've always been so nice to me."

"Father Collie, why are you doing this? I'm a nun; you're a priest. Just because it's trendy right now for members of the cloth to get involved with each other, it doesn't mean that we all have to." I'm such a hypocrite. "Now, please, Will, I'm trying to enjoy the party and you really are spoiling it for me. I don't want what you're suggesting. Please forget this."

"I can't. I love you." His eyes are damp, his face contorted in pain.

Oh, God, don't cry, Will.

"Well, sorry, I don't want to hurt you but I don't love you. Now I really don't care to continue this discussion." I walk away. It is not easy for either of us to enjoy the rest of the party. If I didn't have to wait for a drive, I'd leave.

A few weeks later he accosts me in the school office when I am entering my marks in the central grade books. I repeat what I'd said before and walk away. Eventually, he stops bothering me but this ends the friendship for me.

~ ~ ~

My hypocrisy strikes again when I receive a Christmas card from Kyle, still chaste, friendly with a certain ambiguity attached. I wonder what he really thinks of me. He quotes Joan Baez, the popular singer: "You – special, miraculous, unrepeatable, fragile, fearful, tender, lost, sparkling, ruby-emerald jewel, rainbow-splendoured person." My heart races. If Kyle weren't halfway across the country, he would have been a greater threat to what remains of my commitment. I can't afford to phone him and he doesn't phone me. Letters are our only form of communication. He's teaching in a Catholic school in New Jersey. It wouldn't surprise me if he became a priest like Fitz. I don't want to tempt him but the words he copied onto the page wrap me like a cozy quilt. I must be loveable – Will and Kyle seem to think so anyway.

~ ~ ~

One task that helps the winter months pass is applying for graduate schools. Sister Bonita gives me permission to do so, since the community continues to pay for my education. I'm eager to start working on a master's degree in drama next summer. I dream of Berkeley and Stanford, prestigious universities with plenty of political unrest. Instead, the University of Kansas in Lawrence accepts me. Bland, except for the tornadoes – there's no place like home! – and unfortunately, I don't have any red shoes to click together. But the theatre department has an excellent academic reputation. And my good friend Fitz from St. John's, soon to be ordained a priest, lives there, so I won't be completely alone.

Chapter XXIX

Tested

In the spring I ask permission to attend a weekend theatre convention in St. Paul. I'll be able to take the bus and spend two nights with Maureen, back from the Peace Corps and teaching there. She has long-range plans for both evenings but Barnabas, now calling himself Roy, since he's leaving, meets me. It is a warm spring night. We stroll along the Mississippi in one of the city's lovely parks. Stars sparkle like blasts of distant fireworks. Roy spreads his jacket so we can sit on the damp grass.

"So my days at St. John's are about over – just another month or so."

"Gosh, you're really leaving the order, being released from your vows. Are you sad about it?"

"Nope," he says offhandedly. "The Church must experience a huge upheaval before all the faithful will finally accept the new values of Vatican II. I have no desire to be part of that chaos. I'm moving on, to teach, maybe to write."

Gulp. He's so matter-of-fact about this life-altering decision. "Are you going to stay with your family in Minneapolis and teach around here?"

"No," he says, rubbing his smooth chin, "I've got a friend who's working in St. Louis and I can probably get a job at the same school. Nah, I want to leave Minnesota altogether and start afresh."

I look down at my lap. "I guess I won't be seeing much more of you then."

"Don't worry, I'll be here until fall and we can always keep writing."

"Sure." I try to hide my surprise. Although I don't feel the physical attraction to him that I felt for Kyle and Patrick, I hate to lose him altogether. Bride of Christ, hmmm?

Then without warning, he gently lays me back on the jacket and begins to kiss me.

One of his arms cushions my back; the other caresses my face. My brain tells me to stop – but the night, the stars, the river, the tingling pleasure throughout my body are too much for my weak will. Words from Solomon's *Canticle of Canticles* sing in my head:

> *Let him kiss me with the kisses of his mouth!*
> *More delightful is your love than wine!*

After ten minutes of serious kissing, I gently push him away, saying, "Maureen will be home soon. I'd better get to her apartment." So with a final kiss on my eyes, he pulls me up and helps me into the car. I check my dress to be sure it has no telltale wrinkles or grass stains.

At her apartment, Maureen and I chat for a while. Then as she did in our girlhood, she hands me down some of her old dresses, still in fine condition, which I can now wear with our revised wardrobes – a two-piece hunter green knit suit and a fabulous navy blue dress with gold buttons. They both look sombre enough to be worn by a nun but I could easily pass for a woman of the world, since I'm no longer wearing either a habit or veil – most of the young sisters adopted this change. I'm behaving like a woman of the world too. I'm ashamed to confess to Maureen what I've been up to. My internal struggle is almost too much to bear.

Lying on her couch that night, I toss and turn, troubled, though excited remembering

Roy's thrilling kisses. Finally, my hand steals downward, tentatively at first, trying to bring back some of the mysterious pleasure that I felt.

After the Saturday seminars, Maureen and I meet at a charming little seafood restaurant where she buys me dinner. She regales me with exotic tales of her travels on the way back from Ethiopia. She is wearing a stunning mini-skirt that she bought in London. Too short for me but I love it. *Très chic* with her leather jacket from Lebanon. I've admired her rug from Greece and her zebra-skin drum from Ethiopia. What an adventure it all was. I feel deprived: deprived of adventure, deprived of freedom, deprived of the full-scale pleasures of a sexual woman.

Maureen has theatre tickets with friends for tonight, booked ages ago but I assure her that I'll be okay. Barnabas – Roy – is coming over again and I'll be fine.

Not exactly – he wants to pick up from where we left off by the river. We hardly talk at all. Almost immediately, he takes off his dark-framed glasses and gets down to business, as if returning to a task left incomplete on his last shift. Suddenly, he is kissing me, circling my breasts with his right hand. He guides my hand to his groin. It is hard. I touch it gingerly – I've never touched a man there before. We keep our clothes on but we certainly know each other more intimately before I finally insist we must pull ourselves together – apart – before Maureen returns.

"Okay but I enjoyed that, didn't you?" He's so casual about it all. I can hardly breathe.

"I don't think you'll last much longer in the convent either."

"Well, not with the likes of you around."

The bus ride back to Eau Claire on Sunday is endless. More of the beautiful poetry of Solomon runs through my guilty head:

> *I adjure you, daughters of Jerusalem*
> *by the gazelles and hinds of the fields,*
> *do not arouse, do not stir up love before its own time.*

We were only kissing, I assure my guilty conscience, but not innocent kisses. I feel cheap for giving into it but I enjoyed it too. I can't focus on my book. I can't even nap. My brain bubbles like a vat of wine.

Chapter XXX

Summer of '69

In the summer of 1969 I take an overnight bus from Minneapolis to Kansas City, then a connecting bus onward to Lawrence, home of the University of Kansas. Clad in a beige light wool suit, the one I wore to my high school graduation, I am reasonably comfortable on the air-conditioned bus, though I can't curl up and sleep. We make a number of stops, but I only get out in Des Moines, Iowa, and Kansas City, Kansas – the major cities – to stretch my legs, and use real bathrooms. Unfortunately they're not much cleaner than the one on the bus. I arrive at 6:00 in the morning to the stillness of stifling heat. The university town is barely awake at this hour. An old tan dog lies in the blue shadow, unmoved by disembarking passengers. I stand waiting in the heat that forces me to remove my jacket. Once all the luggage is unloaded a grim realization hits me – mine has not has not travelled with me. No change of clothing means I'm stuck in this wool suit till the next bus comes in from Minneapolis ten hours from now.

Fitz meets me at the station, his dark hair still falling in his face in the old familiar way. He takes me to the dorm to get settled in. Since I have to register today, there is no choice but to drag myself around in hot clothes – like being a novice again. Fortunately, I do have my toilet articles separate from my missing luggage so at least I can shower and brush my teeth. Once I finish registering which takes most of the day, I phone the bus station. The suitcases have finally arrived.

By now it is late afternoon and Fitz is at work at his father's clothing store, so I take a cab back to the station, pick up my luggage, grab a bite of early supper and sleep for fourteen hours – unquestionably the longest single slumber of my life. I've been losing sleep about my vocation, so spending a night on the bus and a change of scenery seem to be the sedative I need to get caught up.

When I awake, my roommate has arrived. Su Loong is from Thailand and is very shy except in one regard. She doesn't like air conditioning and often returns late at night and turns it off without asking me. I wake up hot and turn it back on again. It is too sultry to have the windows open.

Despite this little disagreement, we become good friends and ironically, she, the "foreigner," brings me into her fold of companions. I spend the summer with the Thais, learning to love their warm natures and spicy food. On Sunday nights, we frequently go to the apartment of some of their married friends for a meal and then for a swim or out to see a film. What a shock for some of them to see a nun in her bathing suit. Though I am now like most of the young nuns, almost exclusively, wearing "street clothes," it's a surprise for them to see so much of my skin exposed.

The Thai students practise Buddhism. It's intriguing for me to meet people so committed to a faith completely different from mine. Unlike Catholicism which always taught us it was the only true religion, Buddhism is very tolerant of other beliefs. The young men in the group were all monks for a couple of years as is common in Thailand. There's no shame in leaving; spending a few years as a monk is standard practice for the majority. It is a way for poorer boys to get an education. I see similarities to my own situation.

A wave of guilt floods over me. Surely I didn't just join the convent for a free education? No, have I forgotten? God called me. I'm one of the chosen ones and besides, I've already taught three years, which earns the community money that I never see, except for a small allowance. Our salaries are held in common for all of us by our treasurer. I believe I'm paying the community back for all they've given me.

The gang at the theatre department includes me in their activities as well. They're delighted to meet me and curious about having a nun in the department. This brings me a lot of welcome attention. My social life is a whirlwind of suppers with new friends and gatherings in the theatre's green room.

One thing that helps me to get to know the library and some of my classmates is a scavenger hunt related to the theatre which sends us to every part of the library, including the closed stacks, reached by a service elevator, unaccompanied by a librarian. Working alone in this remote area seems rather dangerous, a possible opportunity for sexual assault. I never used to worry about things like that. Now I know more about men and their urges. Not to mention my willingness to give into them. What can I do? It is a course requirement. I finish the hunt unscathed but my mind continues to ferment.

~ ~ ~

On the Fourth of July, a couple of weeks after we arrive, we have a huge barbecue supper outside our dormitory dining room. It is another opportunity to meet people. The dessert is watermelon. There are dozens of ripe and juicy fruit, bright red interiors with green striped skin, a sign of summer's abundance. There are pans functioning as spittoons so that seed spitters can do their business. What fun. Not something we would do in the convent. After dark a crowd of us walk to the top of the hill and watch the spectacular fireworks display being held at a sports field.

I love being a co-ed again, an aspect of life I had missed before my year at St. Benedict's. Once again, I feel an urgency to cut loose the bonds of religious life. In so many ways it is a safe, secure way to exist. Yes, we are doing a lot of good for God and His people but I'm starting to think it's not the way I want to spend the rest of my life. Practicing poverty at home was one thing but here I have a very small allowance. There are lots of things on which I could spend my money, especially the many good films that come to town. A new friend, Sister Janine, from Georgia, suggests that I could earn some extra money proofreading other students' theses. A great idea. It is difficult and tedious work but essentially like marking English papers. I make fifty dollars doing each one. It seems like a fortune. I join friends seeing *Zorba the Greek* and other recently opened films. Afterwards we go out for pizza – like normal co-eds.

Janine and I often talk. She is wavering in her vocation, just as I am and we both hint that in another year perhaps, we will leave our communities but continue our educations here at KU. So if that all comes to pass, if we don't change our minds, we'll be roommates. It is energizing to think that I have a plan – whatever happens.

As I walk along some of the beautifully manicured paths, near the carillon that chimes the hour, I accuse myself of biting the hand that feeds me. The community has given me so many opportunities. Besides, I enjoy my teaching situation at Regis. But I see students involved in PDA, as they call it – public display of affection – behind bushes, on the hillsides, even holding hands across a café table. I envy them. I remember Roy. It's hard to think straight when the humidity clogs my brain.

Most of the time the Kansas sultriness is oppressive. The muggy days are a recipe for tornadoes and on more than one occasion, we have to take cover, as a funnel is sighted moving our way. All the co-eds are jammed into the basement of Naismith Hall for an hour or two until the storm literally blows over. What did we expect? Lawrence is a mere thirty miles away from Topeka, the tornado capital of the U.S.

~ ~ ~

On July 20, the U.S. safely completes its first moon landing. The days leading up to this are full of anticipation. We need to beat the Russians on this one; it's a matter of national pride. I'm thrilled to sit in the lounge with many other students, cheering on our nation's success. We showed those Russians. "One small step for a man, one giant leap for mankind," as Neil Armstrong said when he walked on the moon. It's such an exciting time to be alive. The possibilities for adventure and exploration are endless. I long to be a part of all the great new developments in the world. Being tied to the community makes me feel stifled, restricted. The never-ending waves of guilt return.

~ ~ ~

As the summer school session ends, I leave for Wisconsin, uncertain of the direction my future will take. Roy, now a layman, meets me at the bus. I'm not in love with him but he keeps me on edge with his signs of interest. He is settling into a new life, staying at his family home in Minneapolis till he leaves to teach at a college in St. Louis in the fall.

He drives me home to Mother's farm where I am to spend a week before going back to Regis. Mother is naturally curious as to why a man has brought me home. I brush off her questions.

"He's just a friend. He lives in the Cities and has time on his hands till the fall semester begins."

She accepts my answer but I sense she suspects there's more going on than I've told her. Mother's life as a struggling widow is far from enviable, yet I even envy her at times. And I'm painfully jealous of Sandy and Rita, with all their adorable little children. No doubt they feel dragged down at times by the choice they have made but they have freedoms I long to have. Mostly I envy them their children. I long to be more than just a bride of Christ.

Rita invites us to her house for a picnic supper. Her friendly neighbour, Eloise, not a Catholic, is delighted when she hears that I am coming.

"Invite me over to meet her, please. I've never actually met a nun."

Of course, when Eloise is actually introduced to me, she's a little surprised and maybe even disappointed that I'm not wearing a habit and that I'm pretty down-to-earth with a sense of humour not unlike Rita's. She can't believe that I like hamburgers with relish and mustard and that I don't turn down chocolate ice cream for dessert.

When Rita calls the next day and tells me Eloise was amazed that I was so undistinguished, I have to laugh. I know and Rita knows that I am still an ordinary person though I did try to act the role of a celebrity when I met her friend. With all that is going on in my brain, I feel a fake, an impostor. People imagine that becoming a nun automatically makes a person holy but I realize that it would take a lifetime of concentrated effort to achieve that. Some of my older role models, like Sister Freda, Sister Agnes and of course, Mother Dorothy, would have been better examples of the religious life for Eloise to meet.

I'm relieved that Roy is leaving for St. Louis to work with his friend though I have enjoyed all the attention he's paid me. I don't think he really cares any more about me than I do about him, but when he's around I always want to practise that deep kissing again and to feel him caressing my breasts. I know I mustn't.

~ ~ ~

When I return to Regis a couple of weeks before school starts, I'm still weighing matters in my own mind. Despite my growing independence, now that I'm back with the community, I feel trapped. I call Megan and Bonnie to get their views on whether to leave or to stay. They are both staying put but Bonnie is sympathetic.

"You have to make up your own mind," she says. "It's your life but as for me, this is still a good way to live."

Fair enough.

Megan isn't so easy on me.

"Bridge, I can't believe that God's most perfect little nun is thinking of leaving Him. Jumpin' on the bandwagon of deserters, are you?" she accuses me with a snicker.

"It's not funny. It's very serious. I don't know what to do. My indecisiveness is making me more and miserable. Sister

Suzanne hated quitters and she left. I don't know. I always told you I wasn't perfect and if anything, I'm getting worse. Enough of this. It's too depressing. I'll talk to you again soon. Bye."

Chapter XXXI

Stormy Weather

Even though my life as a nun is in flux, I've finally got the knack of teaching and have many satisfying moments in my second year at Regis. Many of last year's Junior drama class and my Junior English students form the core of my Senior drama class. It's energizing to start planning the fall children's show with them.

We decide to mount *The Pied Piper of Hamelin* and we only have one piper, one large cast. The Piper role is an obvious choice: the tall, skinny joker who always keeps me on my toes, Tom W. He learns the part quickly and causes me no trouble. Because Steve D. has graduated, I feel somewhat bereft. But Mary and Cathy quickly take over the technical roles which interest them more than acting – unusual but a godsend.

While the rest of us rehearse, Donna, Linda and Candy are in charge of the rat brigade. They stuff used pantyhose and decorate these little creatures with eyes and whiskers – no blind mice for us. Then they string them together and as Tom pipes his way in and out of the back drapes, the girls jam the strings into the back of his jeans so that it will look as if the mice were following him out of town. It works convincingly.

The loss of Steve D. also means that we don't have a truck driver, so we keep the set simple and instead of heading out of town, we take the show to a couple of nursing homes in the area, with some students and me driving our cars. At the first one, our performance space is "intimate," to say the least. The students are intimidated by having these aging citizens in various states of health or dementia sitting nearly on top of them. The show progresses reasonably well until one old man in the front row, clearly out of touch with the drama, begins loudly reciting the alphabet. "A", he says loudly, "B", loud and clear, "C. C. C." Oh dear, he is stuck, until someone behind him yells out, "D!" at the top of his lungs.

Despite the interruption, the show must go on – I've drilled it into my students – so somehow they manage to finish without collapsing in laughter. We make up for it in the cars on the way back to school. The second outside performance is better and by the time we perform on Saturday and Sunday at Regis for the kids of the city, we are brilliant. Everything moves like a perfectly tuned machine. I am so proud of them and love them for their commitment and effort. After the last show they call me up to receive the customary roses. I send them home with lots of hugs and kisses after we've struck the set.

That isn't the end of it for the students. About twenty minutes after settling in to read the paper in the community room, I hear the side doorbell ring. Sister Joan answers it and I hear a voice that is surely Tom asking, "Can Sister Bridget come out to play?" I hurry to the door.

We go across the street to Mother's Pizza for a celebratory supper of pizza washed down by? Pitchers of beer! Of course, we are all old enough to drink beer in Wisconsin but I'm a nun. These are my high school students. This is irregular behaviour and I feel uneasy when, just as I lift a slice of pizza to my mouth, the pitcher of beer right in front of me, someone snaps a photo. The shock and surprise are permanently registered on my face.

~ ~ ~

The post-production blues are dispelled with an invitation from St. Benedict's to bring some of my students to a Saturday matinee of the Christmas opera, *Amahl and the Night Visitors*. It's a long drive, nearly three and a half hours at the best of times and this is the beginning of winter. I worry that anything can happen. When I present the opportunity to my drama classes, some of the girls are eager to go. For one thing, it's a chance for them to check out the college as a future place for them to study. Linda, Candy, Donna and Cathy pay for their tickets and we make plans for the first Saturday of December.

As we leave the school at 8:00 in the morning, light flakes of snow are just beginning to fall. By the time we reach the outskirts of the Twin Cities, it is snowing heavily. The grey Pontiac has seen better days but it's solid and holds the road pretty well. At least, that is, until we reach a barren wasteland halfway between the Cities and the college. Not a building or service station in sight. Suddenly, we hit a slick spot and spin in a complete circle. We're all terrified, but luckily the girls don't scream at me. Perhaps they're too scared to make a sound. There's little traffic and I have time to right the Pontiac without incident. I proceed with greater caution. Despite our scare we arrive safely at St Benedict's. It feels good to be back after more than a year away. When I go over to the Motherhouse to let them know we're there, they invite us to have lunch in the nuns' cafeteria. Appealing aromas of chicken stew and homemade bread lure us in for a hearty meal.

The theatre crowd lets me show the girls around all the nooks and crannies of the department before the show begins. The girls are impressed. We totally enjoy the play and have trouble not singing along with the familiar songs such as, "Do You See What I See?"

When the show ends, I'm ready to set out quickly, because the storm has worsened and I know it will take a long time to get home. But Sister Colman, my former professor and advisor, calls me over in the theatre lobby.

"Sister, someone at the Motherhouse has just checked with the highway department. Road conditions all along 694 and 94 have deteriorated since noon. They're recommending that people stay off the roads until they can be cleaned once the storm lets up. I think you'd better stay here tonight."

"Oh but the girls' families will have to be notified and Regis and..."

"Don't worry, you can make those calls in a minute. We'll put you up in the girls' dorm near the theatre. Do you mind sharing a room with one or two of the girls?"

Hmmm. We have brought nothing extra along, so I guess I'll have to sleep in my slip. The girls should find that amusing. But what can we do? The highways are all but closed so we have to make the best of a bad situation.

After dinner, we check out our rooms. Donna and I will share one room and the other girls, a second one. A little like being a junior sister again. We watch a film at the theatre department that night, *Cat Ballou* with Jane Fonda. She's a wild, independent woman. I admire her, even envy her. The girls and I share some laughs, taking our minds off the fact that we're snowbound.

There's no point in pretending I'm anything but an ordinary woman, so I undress in the bathroom and come out in my slip. I slide quickly into bed and Donna has discreetly turned her head during these moments. There's a knock on our door and Donna, still dressed, opens it. It's Candy, Linda and Cathy. They pile onto my bed as if it were a pajama party.

"Sister, what made you enter the convent? Didn't you like boys?" Linda asks.

"Of course I liked boys; I had my share of boyfriends. But I felt God was calling me."

"Calling you?" Candy wondered. "How did you hear this call?"

"Hard to explain. Just a belief that God wanted me to do something good for the world and if I didn't I'd regret it all my life."

"But," Cathy asked, "don't you ever wish you had a husband and children of your own?" This cuts close to the heart of the matter.

"Girls, in short, I am a normal woman with normal desires. Of course, I'd like all those things you talk about but I've given them up for God. Now, off to bed with you. I, for one, need to get some sleep, because it's probably going to be a long and challenging drive home tomorrow. So, skedaddle."

"Yes, Sister," they say, giggling and rush off.

"By the way, nice slip!" Cathy yells, cheekily, as she leaves the room. I shake my head, grinning.

Trying to fall asleep, I mull over what I've told the girls and wonder if I'm misleading them. Donna is soon breathing evenly, fast asleep. Finally, I nod off.

It's ten o'clock the next morning before the roads are declared safe for travelling. We've attended Mass and enjoyed a healthy breakfast. The drive home is longer than usual but in fact, the roads are in much better shape than they were on the way up because the storm is over and they've been plowed.

At four o'clock in the afternoon, after dropping the girls off at their homes, I finally drive toward the garage at Regis. Our parking lot hasn't been cleared very well and just outside the garage entry ironically enough, I get stuck. I lock the old Pontiac and leave it for later. I've had enough adventures for one weekend.

~ ~ ~

Once the main events of Christmas are over, I am able to go to my family's home for a week. Christmas at Regis has not measured up to my Christmas as a novice. Nobody puts much effort into preparing her gift; I get two by mistake. Then we discover that Sister Georgia doesn't have any and she cares very little about this fact. I let her choose one of mine – they are not memorable, anyway.

~ ~ ~

It's good to get back to my mother's farm. By now, only Terry is living at home; Teresa and Maureen both married quietly this year. They are studying or teaching. Mother has all the Christmas treats that I love – especially rosettes and Grandma-style sugar cookies. There are some peanut butter ones with the Hershey's kiss in the centre from Aunt Shelley and some of Grandma's specialties with the date filling. I pig out. Maybe all that sugar will help me come to a satisfactory decision about my future.

Mother has noticed that I am less lively, more introspective than usual. One night after supper, we sit across from each other in our familiar spots in the living room. She is in her big chair; I'm curled up on the couch with a book. Terry is out with friends. The lights of the Christmas tree throw eerie shadows on the room.

"Is everything all right?" she asks. "You don't seem yourself."

I sigh deeply. I have to share this with her eventually. What better time than now, since she has opened this door. How to begin?

"Well, Mom, I know that I have changed in the last couple of years. Being at St. Benedict's was a big part of it but in fact, even before that, I felt rather unsettled in the religious life."

"So what, then, are you going to leave like all these nuns and priests that we hear about all the time?" She sounds worried, maybe even angry.

A direct hit! A palpable hit! Until she asked the question, I had not been sure of the answer.

I lower my head, as if confessing, "Yes, I probably am. I'm certainly leaning in that direction."

"Are you involved with that Roy who drove you home last summer?"

I blush a little. "No, I'm not. We write and he has come to visit me a few times but I'm not in love with him – or with anyone at the moment."

"At the moment? So you have been, since you've been in the convent? You've been in love with men?" Her voice rises in amazement.

"I'm not sure I understand that kind of love. I think my attractions were pretty adolescent, probably growing out of what feels more and more like an unnatural deprivation. Mom, I'm twenty-six. The other girls in the family were all married by my age, except for Maureen and she's married now, too. Rita and Sandy have those adorable children. I want a child. It's an overwhelming longing. I can't seem to get past it."

"Having children is no picnic, you know. It's hard work, a constant struggle, especially if your husband isn't very reliable about supporting you." She chokes up. "Married life is no bed of roses." Her voice breaks and tears well in her eyes.

I speak quietly. "Mom, I know that your life hasn't been easy but I want to find my own new way to live. I've got an education now and I can teach, so I'll never have to rely on a man to support me. My life will be different from yours."

Mother slumps back in her chair and sighs. "I'm sorry to hear you talking this way, Karen," she says slowly. I can hear the pain in her voice. Then shaking her head, she adds, "But it is your life and whatever you decide to do, I guess I have to accept it."

That was Mom. She always did that, with all her children. She might feel sad and disappointed with our decisions – she obviously did now – but she stood by us through our mistakes and our triumphs.

I try to soften the blow. "I know it won't be easy, Mom, but this no longer feels right. So I'll soon be writing a letter to the Pope asking for a dispensation."

"The Pope? I thought the Bishop could grant dispensations. Other nuns seem get them from the Bishop according to *The Times Review*."

"Yes, it's true but Benedictines are a papal order, so only the Pope can dissolve our vows. It's a legal matter, really, like getting a divorce."

"Well, let's keep this in the family until you actually leave, okay? This is a small town and people gossip. I'm the one who has to live and work here."

I feel a little let down that she is so business-like about this. But it's a shock for her. She hasn't been privy to my internal struggles, so she's been taken unawares. I'm sure she will stand by me in the end.

"Don't worry, Mom, I'll keep it in the family." I walk over to her and give her a gentle hug. She picks up the newspaper, perhaps to hide any tears. I turn back to my book. How cold I have become about this subject; I can't even cry. Still, I'm relieved that Dad isn't around or I'd have to tell him, too.

~ ~ ~

Fortunately, I can tell Grandma, who will be ecstatic with the news. The next afternoon, as another snowfall begins, Mom and I stop in at Grandma's for a little visit. The aroma of her sugar cookies presses a button of nostalgia in my heart. When we sit down in the crowded living room with the smelly old oil stove, I admire a beautiful quilt that she is working on for Maureen and Tom as a belated wedding gift. A justice of the peace married them in October with no fanfare. My heart catches thinking of their joy and the life that will take place beneath their log cabin patterned quilt. I long to tell someone about the restlessness that is driving my life.

"I love your quilts, Grandma. It would be so nice to have forever, something that you made with your own hands. Will you please make me one, when you finish this one?"

Grandma, a tough old bird who never approved of my chosen vocation, says bluntly, "I'll start making you a quilt when I hear that you're leaving the convent."

"Well, Grandma, you can start making my quilt!"

"What do you mean?" I've surprised her as much as I did Mom. "You mean you're not going back there anymore?"

"It's not a prison, Grandma and of course, I have to go back and finish the school year. But I think I'll be leaving when school is out at the end of May."

"When did you decide this?"

"Just recently. I only told Mom yesterday." Mom nods, her face grim, resigned to my decision. "We're going to keep it in the immediate family until I leave. You know how people gossip and Mom doesn't want that."

Grandma gets up and hobbles over to me, despite arthritic back and knees, enfolding me in a big hug. "I'm so glad," she said. "I always thought the convent was a waste of your good brain and spunkiness. I'll start your quilt soon."

That was easier than I expected. It is almost a physical pain at times, thinking of leaving the people at St. Anselm's whom I have grown to love. I admire so many of them but I'm not happy anymore. There is a growing void in my life that the community no longer fills. My fault, not theirs – or maybe, no one's fault.

On Saturday morning the snow is very heavy, blowing and drifting. Mom goes to work for a couple of hours but even her stingy boss can see that no one will be coming in to town to shop on a day like this. She picks up a few groceries, so we are ready to be snowed in for a while. It's cozy in the house and I have the couch, an afghan and the massive weight of *Anna Karenina* to keep me content. Not to mention all those leftover Christmas cookies.

I'm lost in the story of Anna's passionate love affair with Vronsky. I shake my head at her decision. How could she give up her child for a man?

I'm brought back to reality as the phone rings. Mother answers it. "Yes, it is. Yes she is. We're about four miles from where you are. Here, I'll let you talk to Sister Bridget."

"Who is it?" I ask.

Raising her eyebrows, she says, "Some priest. He says he's a friend of yours from St. Benedict's."

I pick up the receiver. "Hi, this is Sister Bridget."

"Bridget! It's Larry Indigo. I've been to see Stef in St. Cloud and the gang at St. John's and I was headed to Stephen's Point to see John. But this storm is making for hazardous driving. Visibility is very poor. According to your mother, I'm only a few miles away from you right now."

"Where are you and how did you get Mother's number?" This is bizarre.

"Actually, I remembered your mother from your graduation from St. Benedict's and I just looked it up in the phone book. It's a fluke that I caught you during your visit. I'm up at the Woodville exit, just north of Spring Valley, so it appears. I wondered if I could come to your mom's and maybe ride out the storm for a few hours."

Curious. Larry is another priest who finds me more attractive than I find him and besides, I really have no desire to get involved with a priest. That will complicate my situation even more. Still here he is, a mere four miles away and hoping to find shelter from the blizzard. "Of course, Larry, come on out to the farm. Now here's the way to get here . . ."

After hanging up, I quickly explain what is happening. Mother, who has picked up the gist of this from what I was saying on the phone, is already tidying up and thinking of what to have for lunch.

"He'll probably have to spend the night if the storm continues. So you'd better check on the condition of the spare room and put some fresh sheets on the bed."

"Oh, do you think. . .?" I start then realize that she is right and race upstairs to prepare a room. With the bad weather, the short ride takes Larry nearly twenty minutes. By the time he arrives, the house is in order and a pot of fresh coffee is brewing.

Mom met Larry once before on the day of my graduation, a busy day when she was introduced to so many strangers that she hardly knows him. But she welcomes him like a family member and he responds graciously to her warmth.

We enjoy a wonderful lunch that day and lots of chatter. Terry calls home to say he's staying in River Falls with friends due to the storm.

While Mother is fixing dinner, which she insists on doing alone, Larry and I get caught up on the other people we know in common. Eventually Roy's name comes up. They were grad students together.

"Yes, I haven't heard from him in a while, though we spent some time together last summer. I know he's working in St. Louis. He said he had a friend there."

Larry drops a bombshell. "That friend is the former Sister Carlene, whom you must have met at St. John's. They both left their orders and from what I hear, they're living together."

The shock must be evident on my face. Even though I knew Roy and I had drifted apart, I hadn't realized he was so involved with a woman. Naturally, I'd assumed his friend was a man, an ex-monk or something. I didn't really know Sister Carlene but it doesn't matter. The effect is the same either way. I can only nod while I try to regain my equilibrium. Fortunately, Mom calls us to dinner soon and I try to forget about Roy in the camaraderie of the moment. Not a bad way to wait out a Wisconsin winter storm.

The next morning, the snow has stopped and Larry goes out to start both his car and Mother's. Unfortunately, Mom's battery is dead, so Larry jump-starts her car and leaves it running, while he offers Mass in her dining room. Mother, a devout convert, is thrilled with this. When she gives Larry his farewell hug, it is heartfelt.

~ ~ ~

The rest of the holiday is uneventful by comparison. Back at Regis, we are having furnace problems as we always seem to during holidays. The convent is connected to the school, and when the thermostat is lowered at school, it's difficult to keep things comfortable in the convent. Professional heating consultants are enlisted to solve the problem but we spend a couple of days wrapped in our heaviest clothes trying to keep warm.

One day near the end of vacation I receive a package postmarked Garwood, New Jersey. It is a late Christmas gift from Kyle, *The Little Prince* by Antoine de Saint Exupéry. This book has been a popular one among university students and also among people in the religious life. I first read it in French class with Monsieur Du Villes. There are so many lines in the book that punctuate the special friendship I have with Kyle. "I have made him my friend and now he is unique in all the world... It is only with the heart that one can see rightly; what is essential is invisible to the eye... It is the time you have wasted for your rose that makes your rose so important... You become responsible, forever, for what you have tamed. You are responsible for your rose."

Dear, sweet Kyle. I read the book over and over. There is so much food for thought here. I look up at the bookshelf above the desk in my room. From Larry, the book on *Love and Sexuality*, from Roy, Hesse's *Steppenwolf* – deep philosophy. Roy's change of status upsets me more than I care to admit. I feel sad that he moved in with a woman without even telling me. But Kyle's choice of book speaks to my heart, reminding me of the valuable friendships I have formed in the community and beyond. It cheers me up.

~ ~ ~

Perhaps some exercise will bring me out of my pensive state. There's a lot of snow to move. Faith and I keep our shovels far apart this winter, not wanting a repeat of my black eye. The banks are higher than the cars on the other side of the street. Faith and I spend a lot of time skating and discussing our future plans. She knows that I am planning to leave. She is wavering herself. Like me, she can't seem to get over longing for a man in her life and she continues to have a number of curious phone calls which she wouldn't want everyone to know about. On the other hand, like me, she values community life. We are a couple of crazy, mixed-up kids.

Chapter XXXII

In Bed With Bonnie Again

It is the Sunday before we are to go back to school. The building is still too cold for real comfort but we are warmed up by a lunchtime visit with some of the sisters from La Crosse. This means that Bonnie is here. I have been dying to see her. Long distance calls are still expensive and discouraged. So we have to make the most of our infrequent visits.

Lunch is lively with bright chatter, catching up on each other's activities. The old community spirit is very much in evidence and momentarily, I wonder if I will be making a mistake by leaving. Once everything is cleared away, Bonnie and I go up to my room where we can talk in private. Even on the missions, talking in bedrooms is discouraged. We are supposed to meditate and sleep there, nothing else; people naturally tend to talk about intimate matters in bedrooms. We aren't concerned, though. I, after all, am leaving soon and my adherence to the rules is loosening. Bonnie is my guest. I'll take the blame.

My bedroom is frigid. The wind from the north is howling around the windows. We can actually see our breath. Our chattering teeth make it difficult to carry on a conversation.

At first we huddle in my cape and cloak. Finally Bonnie says, "Why don't we get under the covers? It would be warmer there and we could share body heat."

Good idea. We strip to our slips and crawl into my single bed, cuddling together for warmth, like the sisters that we are. I begin to fill Bonnie in on all that has been happening in my life.

"And so," I say, "I'm going to apply for a dispensation soon."

Like Mother, she does not try to discourage me and she is less surprised than Mother was; Bonnie knew for a while I was wavering. "We'll miss you; I can't imagine life here without you."

"We'll keep in touch, of course. We'll always be friends. Why don't you leave too? You seem to have your share of beefs."

"You know, I appreciate your decision but I have to say that for me, this is still the right place to be. I'll pray. . ."

Suddenly there is a knock on the door. Feeling mostly innocent – except for all the talking – I say calmly, "Come in!"

Sister Augusta, a dear old soul in her 80's, opens the door. When she sees us in bed together, her hand covers her mouth and she looks away.

"Oh, Sister," I say, quickly grasping what she must think, "we're just trying to keep warm."

"Of course," she says, shaking her head rapidly, nervously. "Well, I just wanted to let you know that the heat is on and it's quite warm in the community room now."

"Okay, thanks, Sister, we'll be right down."

As she closes the door, Bonnie and I burst into muffled laughter.

~ ~ ~

I turn the pages of *The Godfather*, intently visualizing the sexual activities of Sonny Corleone and his girlfriend. It sounds violent, frightening, thrilling. It turns me on. As I imagine him ripping off her panties, my own right hand strays to my nightie, which I gently pull upward. My head is full of warnings and guilt. I set the heavy book on my groin. The weight reminds me of Roy on the spring evening in St. Paul. My left hand slips inside the top of my flannel nightie, teasing my nipple into firmness. One warm finger of my right hand slips into a now-familiar channel, slowly and gently at first, and gradually becoming more urgent as the pleasure grows. Friction wins out and my pelvis rises as I try to experience every ounce of gratification. At last the explosion comes. My state of ecstasy is complete. I swallow my moans. Aaah. Once again, I feel the relief of not being caught in the act. Jesus knows, of course. What must He think of His bride? He knows I'm going to be a dropout soon. Will He punish me, as I probably deserve, as the priests and nuns used to warn? Fortunately, my body is totally exhausted from its workout or I would never fall asleep. I set the book on the bedside table and turn out the lamp.

Chapter XXXIII

Making It Official

My strange state of mind continues as we return to school after the Christmas holidays. I analyze everything that happens in the community, trying to convince myself that the decision to leave religious life is the right one for me. Bonnie's comments about the positive aspects of our life rang some bells for me too. I wonder if I am just taking the easy way out. In many ways, it is a relief to get back to work because I get caught up in preparing and presenting lessons, working on minor plays. I have less time to focus on what is coming after the semester ends.

Some of the drama students are begging me to organize a debating team. I've dealt with other types of public speaking but never debate, so even though I know nothing about it, with more courage than sense I agree to organize one. Something more to keep my brain busy and away from my self-imposed turmoil. Together we learn the rigorous format and begin to practise two afternoons a week after school. Dave, future lawyer, Cathy, Mary and Gene are the heart of the group. Their keenness is contagious. Soon we're on the school debate circuit and occasionally even winning.

Along with that, I continue to coach forensics, the type of competitive speech activities that I have always loved, and one of my own strengths. With a large group of keen participants, this takes up quite a lot of my free time after school. I rarely return to the convent till just before evening prayers. Little by little, my life becomes more involved with my students than with my community. I feel much more comfortable and at home with them than I do with the nuns. We are much closer in age, except for Faith and Joan, who are still my good buddies. How I miss the camaraderie that was part of life as a junior sister at the Priory.

Am I just immature? Will I be able to make a greater impact on the world when I leave? With all the foment in the country surrounding the struggle for equal rights for blacks and the protests against the Vietnam war, I want to play a bigger role in the world.

On Sundays, some of us begin attending services at the various parish churches in Eau Claire, of which there were several. Our community is encouraging us to share more in the life of the general community and to become more involved in parish life. For me, this only serves to cement my view that the laity are perhaps better servants of God than we are.

Again I see Mrs. Shea with her six children and stand in awe of all that she, a widow, is contributing to church life. She teaches catechism, organizes fundraisers and leads Bible studies. All of this as well as the commitment to her family. I convince myself that she and other lay people are doing a much better job of serving Christ's people than we nuns are – or at least than I am. Yet at the end of the day, they have their families to go home to. The sisters at Regis with a few exceptions don't really feel like family, just colleagues.

~ ~ ~

One Sunday afternoon in early spring, I receive a phone call from a voice in the recent past.

"Bridget, is that you? How are you?"

"Kyle? Kyle Craig? Where are you calling from?" In spite of myself I feel hot; my whole body tingles. I blush in the little phone booth in the corridor that offers me some privacy.

"Actually, I'm calling from the rest area just southeast of Eau Claire, off the interstate. I'm headed toward St. John's to see friends and wondered if you're not too busy, whether I could stop in for a short visit?"

There is no disguising my delight. "Omigod, yes, that would be great! Which exit is it? Let me tell you how to get here."

Within twenty minutes, he is at the front door of the convent, blonde and irresistible, ready to tap dance into some fun.

"This is so great, Kyle," I say, hugging him. "I'm really glad to see you again after so long. Come sit down and tell me what you're up to." I lead him into one of the visiting rooms not far from the chapel. We sit at right angles to each other, close but not close enough to touch.

"Well, as I mentioned at Christmas, I've been teaching English at an inner city school in Garwood. The kids are really needy but I love them and I think they quite like me."

"I'm sure they do. I'll bet you play your guitar for them."

"Every chance I get. I stay after school for a couple of hours every day, organizing improvisations and music with the children."

"Typical. I knew your heart was in the arts. Where are you living?"

"It's close to home, so for a while, I'm living with my folks."

"No girlfriend to share with then?" I tease.

"Oh no, lots of friends, as usual but no one special. I still think of entering the priesthood, like Fitz."

"Do you? You don't think you're doing as much good as a layman?" I can't resist raising my favourite question.

"I don't know. What do you think? Look at all the good you're doing. Could you do that if you weren't a nun?"

"Yes, I think I could. I see the good that lay people do and I wonder. I admit I've become rather disenchanted with the religious life." I don't add – you were part of that. I don't want to reignite the old fires here.

"Umm, is there a guy. . . ?"

"No, no one special." I hesitate, thinking of my former attachment to him, of which I still believe he was unaware. "I do seem to be attracted to men all the time which makes me feel guilty. If I were a layperson, I could do good without having to feel ashamed all the time. When I think of all that my mom does, for instance. . ." I pause, looking down at my hands.

"So, it sounds as if you're not going to stay," he says, crestfallen. "I'm sorry to hear it. I admired you so much as a nun. I find it safe to become friends with nuns and priests, since they don't seem to be trying to get involved with me in a conjugal way. You know? Well, whatever happens, I hope life works out for you." I raise my eyebrows during this speech; it confirms what I've often thought about him.

We catch up quickly on all our other acquaintances and then, he has to rush off. As he pulls away, I ponder again whether I am doing the right thing. I've never felt so torn before. No, I insist to myself, leaving still seems right.

~ ~ ~

The following week, I drive to the Priory to see Mother Dorothy one day after school. I need to talk to her and to begin making official application to be released from my vows.

She stands up as I enter and welcomes me with a warm hug, as always. Her kindness makes my revelation at once easier and harder.

"Sister Bridget, I'm sorry to hear of your decision. I sensed that things haven't been right for a while. Is it life at Regis, or have you fallen in love with someone, as it seems the fashion to do these days?"

"No, Mother. Though honestly, I do find the vow of chastity very difficult to keep."

She nods a little. "No one ever told you this would be easy, did they?"

"No, Mother, they didn't. I know that things can be tough on the outside too. Believe me, my own mother's life has hardly been enviable. And no, it's not really Regis, though I admit life there is very different from the Priory or Altoona. Community life takes a back seat to people's personal activities. I think when I had a rich communal life I found the practice of the vows easier. I don't know – I'm not really explaining myself very well but I've thought this over carefully and I'm sure that I want to apply for a dispensation."

She stands upright, speaking coolly. But I can see her eyes watering.

"Well, Sister, I won't try to make you change your mind but I am sorry that you'll be leaving. People at Regis speak well of you and your work. They say you get along well with everyone."

I bow my head to hide the tears that well up in my own eyes. "Thanks for your understanding, Mother. I – I want you to know that I've always had the greatest respect for you personally. You've been like a mother to me."

"Thank you, I've always sensed that." She pats my hand and reaches into her desk to retrieve a form. "Now, here's the outline of what you have to do. I'll pray that you're making the right decision."

"Yes, please do."

I send off the letter to the Pope, as I am required to do, with another copy for the Bishop of our diocese and a third for Mother Dorothy. There is no turning back now.

~ ~ ~

At the end of the month, we all gather at the Motherhouse for a business meeting. After lunch, there is a little break, so Bonnie and I wander into the cloisters for a private chat. Sun streams through the many windows, illuminating the rays of dust. We sit on a bench in front of some of them. The words are slow to come.

"Well, I've done the deed," I say.

"What do you mean, you've talked to Mother?"

"Yes, that and I've written and sent off the required letters. The die is cast."

"Well, ever since Christmas, I've been thinking of our conversation in your bedroom."

I twinkle a little and we smother a giggle. "You mean the one where Sister Augusta caught us in bed together?"

She smiles. "Yeah, right. Anyway, this may come as a surprise to you but your words made a lot of sense to me as I thought them over. And it's true, community life at the larger missions isn't much like it was when we were here."

"And so. . . ?"

"And so, I'm going to talk to Mother, too, about leaving."

I burst into tears. "Oh no, Bonnie, I hope I haven't been a bad influence on you. You helped me so much in the early days. Oh, God, Mother knows we're good friends. She'll think I've led you astray."

"Oh relax," she says, calmly as ever. "This is my decision.

You didn't talk me into anything. Maybe your decision just acted as a catalyst for me in making mine. But it's been coming. I've been thinking about all this for a long time, too. This is not your fault. I just realized how much I agreed with what you said. So now, give me a hug and be happy for me."

I do as she asks. There is a part of me that aches for the community losing so many young sisters and gaining very few in return. And while my leaving has begun to make sense to me, it will be quite a while before I come to terms with Bonnie's departure from St. Anselm's.

Nevertheless, we can't help feeling upbeat when we meet up with Megan later that afternoon. She can tell by our conspiratorial looks that something is going on.

"What have you two been up to?"

With a glance at each other, we burst into the Peter, Paul and Mary hit, *"We're leavin' on a jet plane. . ."*

"What does that mean? Where are you going? Can I come too?"

"Only if you're ready to leave the community," I whisper.

Her face falls. Here is Megan, the rabble-rouser and rebel who has always broken every rule and she is the one who is still committed to the vows we all made.

"You're leaving the community. And you didn't tell me?"

"We're telling you. We wanted to do the official stuff first. But you're among the first to know."

"Oh, sure, go off and leave me with. . . you can't go!"

"Oh yes we can," I say, "but you could come too and anyway, we'll always, always be friends.

"Yeah but not sisters anymore, right?" Megan, who seldom weeps publicly, sheds copious tears and Bonnie and I grab her and share her grief. Suddenly, Peter, Paul and Mary don't seem so funny. The family is falling apart. With the best will in the world, we know that our relationships will never be the same once some of us leave the convent. We love each other but we'll travel our own roads and they may seldom cross.

Chapter XXXIV

Anti-War Demonstrations

As spring is burgeoning, my personal turmoil is echoed in the outside world. At universities all over America, students are holding anti-Vietnam war demonstrations. Most of them end with teargas and arrests. But on one otherwise sparkling spring day, at Kent State University in Ohio, tragedy occurs. Four students die as police fire into the crowd to disperse the protestors. Suddenly, America begins to feel like a police state, where the right to protest is quelled by bullets. Our own students can't stop talking about it; we are all sad and outraged. Ironically, we want to fight back.

A couple of weeks later, it is time for me, as advisor of the forensics competitors, to drive a group of students to the State meet at the University of Wisconsin in Madison. These five students qualified to compete against the finest student speakers from across the state. It is a pleasant, sunny day as we are driving down but about halfway, definitely in the middle of nowhere, we have an incident with one of the tires. A retread has worn away and flown off. Fortunately, we are able to limp our way to a gas station where a friendly mechanic pumps up the spare and replaces the damaged tire. We are able to drive away without too much delay but I'm unnerved and wonder whether we will be able to finish our round trip on this mediocre spare.

The students, five of my favs, Donna, Cathy, Mary, Tom and Dave, who have worked on so many plays and other dramatic events with me, find the sense of uncertainty adds to their enjoyment of the journey. They are ebullient, singing and laughing. To calm myself down, I turn on the radio, just as the nine o'clock news announces: "The city of Madison is battening the hatches as a major anti-war demonstration is expected to take place early this afternoon. The University of Wisconsin campus is home to the Dow Chemical Company and is believed to be supplying Agent Orange to the troops in Vietnam. This deadly chemical is being blamed for terrible deaths and injuries, and its long-term effects are still being examined.

"Police have warned shopkeepers and many of them have closed their stores for the day. Drivers are being warned to avoid parking in the downtown core, as the safety of their vehicles cannot be guaranteed."

"Oh my God, what next?" I moan. "You kids are not going to get involved in anything. I'm responsible for your safety. You're all going to have to stick close to me, so that I know you aren't getting into any trouble."

"Aw, come on, Sister B. We're not babies, you know. Some of us are nearly nineteen. We'll be in university next year. We need to learn how to demonstrate," Tom teases me.

"That's fine! Next year, when you're on your own, you can demonstrate up one side of the country and down the other. But, today, when you're supposed to be competing in the state forensics contest, under my supervision, you will not get into any trouble!"

"SHEEESH! Sister Bridget, you're starting to sound like one of the old nuns. We are young adults, you know," Cathy counters acidly.

"And did you want to find your own way home later today?" I say with raised eyebrows.

"Okay, okay, don't threaten. We just wanted to wind you up a little. We'll be as good as gold, right, all?" Cathy asks. Is she winking at the others?

"Right! Yeah! No problem! Okay!" they all chime in.

"Fine, now let's go find a relatively safe place to park on campus, if there is such a thing."

We park, we eat, they perform, some win, some lose. We have a satisfying day. Once we meet up again after the contests have ended, we walk downtown to grab a snack before setting off home. The march took place while the students were competing, so we missed all that drama but in the aftermath, evidence of their violence is everywhere. Targeted shops with broken windows have been looted, cars parked downtown are bashed in and in one particularly amazing and hard-to-imagine situation, a bus lies on its side. We wonder aloud how many people it took to do that.

"See, aren't you glad we missed the demonstration?" I ask them.

"No way," Dave replies. "I wanted to see a real one, not just something on TV."

"Oh, goodness, let's get out of here, before you get into trouble."

We return to the car. As we begin to drive out of town I hear some muffled giggling. As I glance at Tom in the front seat and check the rear view mirror, I notice they are all flashing the peace sign – a minor outbreak of defiance. I just smile and head north.

Chapter XXXV

Wrapping It Up

It is a particularly mild spring and I frequently go for a walk after dinner to get some exercise and to help unscramble my brain, still torn between what I love about being a nun and teaching at Regis and the fact that I simply no longer want to be here. I don't have any good excuse for leaving, except that my desire to be married and to have children is overwhelming. Any book of spiritual reading would point out that such feelings were not uncommon, that the loneliness felt by celibate people is shared by people in happy conjugal relationships. The tainted nature of humanity means that none of us will ever be happy all the time. Still, my mind is made up. The wheels are turning towards my departure.

One afternoon when I check my mailbox, there is a large official-looking envelope. The postmark is from Vatican City. Wonderful stamps. I feel weak, nearly ready to faint. I sit on one of the couches for a moment before walking upstairs to open this important document – my dispensation.

My hands tremble as I slide the letter opener under the sealed flap. Carefully, I extract this vital paper which will change my life forever. My six-weeks course in Latin doesn't qualify me to translate all of it, but I get the gist: *Soror Brigida (Karen Louise) Traynor professa votorum simplicium perpetuorum in Conventu Sororum Benedictionarum in loco v.d. Eau Claire (U.S.A), a Sanctiate Tua humillime implorat indultum saecularizationis,* . . .Yes, Sister Bridget humbly implores to be secularized. And yes, I have been granted a dispensation. It is dated: *Datum Romao, die 21 Aprilis 1970*, and a papal seal is in the lower left corner. I fall back on my bed stunned. I can hardly believe what I have done.

~ ~ ~

One fine evening as I finish my walk, I re-enter the school to pick up some marking that I need to do. As I come down the hall past the little theatre, I notice that all the lights are on. There appears to be some activity underway. I peek in, always a little protective of that area which the drama department uses much of the time. There, setting up audio-visual equipment for a presentation, is my old crush, Father Patrick Gregory, as captivating as ever. I burst into a few bars from "Tears on My Pillow": "You don't remember me but I remember you."

"Of course I remember you," he says, grinning, giving me chaste little hug. "That's right, Bridget, you teach here, don't you?" His infectious grin still makes my stomach flip. A life of celibacy has heightened his attractiveness.

"Yes, I've been here for the past two years. And you're still in La Crosse?"

"Yes, I'm based there but I'm very active in the lay catechetical program now, giving workshops to the laity all over the diocese to help them in their teaching of the catechism. As you know, there are so many people leaving and so few new people entering the religious life that we have to get the laity more involved." He continues to feed his film into the sprockets of the projector.

"The laity certainly accomplish a lot of good here in Eau Claire. I'm so impressed with them and. . . rather envious of their freedom."

He eyes me curiously. "Surely you don't think they're doing more than our own religious members are doing?"

"Actually, I do, to some degree. Some seem even more committed than we are and look," I say, waving a hand, "they go home to their families. We're almost lazy by comparison."

"Aren't you content anymore with being a nun?" he asks.

I pause, "In fact, I'm leaving the convent at the end of the school year. I guess I've lost faith in the superiority of the religious life as a way to serve God."

"Huh. Well, what can I say? I obviously don't agree with you but each of us has to choose according to our own insights. I – uh – well, I hope everything works out for you." I can tell he is uncomfortable and I need to move on.

"Yes, thanks, Father. All the best to you too. You seem serene in your present role in the Church." I move away but turn back to face him as he makes a final comment.

"Yes, I still believe that I can do more good as priest than I could as layman. These are difficult times, I admit, with all the fresh air blowing in on the dusty concepts of the Church. I just think I'd rather ride this wind. I'm looking forward to the next decade and the rejuvenation of the Church. But, to each, his or her own."

"So true," I say, a little sad that we are no longer as connected as we had been when he was a deacon and I a junior sister. "Well, Father, it's been nice seeing you. Your group will be arriving soon, I imagine, and I've got marking to do. So, all the best; maybe we'll meet again sometime."

"Yes, maybe, again good luck." He shakes my hand firmly and I leave the room, just before the predictable tears begin.

Lifting the Veil

~ ~ ~

These days of saying goodbye are difficult. I'm losing sleep. One day I decide I had better talk things over with Sister Bonita, who is my superior at Regis. We are alone in the community room one Sunday afternoon, so I move closer to the couch where she is sitting, reading the Sunday paper.

"May I talk to you for a minute, Sister?" I ask.

"Sure," her chubby cheeks break into her ever-ready smile. "What's up?"

"Well, Sister, you've probably heard rumours that I'm planning to leave the community at the end of May, when school gets out."

She sobers and says, chin in hand, tapping her lip, "Yes, I heard but I hoped it wasn't true. I've been waiting for you to confirm or deny it."

"Yes, it is true." I struggle to explain. "I actually received my dispensation the other day."

Her face clouds over so I continue quickly. "For one thing community life at Regis is so different from Altoona or the Priory. People seem to have the minimum amount of contact with each other. Look at this: it's Sunday afternoon and no one is sitting around visiting. Everyone is just off doing her own thing. We don't play games or put puzzles together. We rarely go for walks as a group."

"But see, you do value the community life. You and people like us could make it better. In fact, it seems to me that you're just about the only one here who gets along with everyone. It's a shame to see you turn your back on it."

She doesn't mince words. Everyone else said, "Well, it's your decision." She is the first one telling me that I am probably making a mistake. I defend myself.

"You know, Sister, I don't really dislike anyone, though

there are some tough characters here. But I'm so envious of young women with children. The Church is changing. Lay people are doing so many good works now. I don't think it's necessary to be a member of the religious community to serve God well."

"Everyone has his or her own way to serve but ours is special. Think of all the glory you brought to Him in the community's production of *Happy Sounds*. Could you see yourself doing something like that as a laywoman?"

"I don't know, Sister, I don't know. I hope I'm not making a terrible mistake but most of the time, I feel that leaving is the right thing for me. I'm awfully independent and I often think that obedience is the toughest vow to keep, though, well, chastity isn't all that easy either."

A blush spreads across her ruddy complexion. Talking about sex isn't something nuns do very often, despite all the rumours to the contrary.

"Ah," she nods. "Are you involved with someone? I've wondered about the number of letters that you get. And phone calls."

"No, Sister, I'm not, though I have been attracted to some men. I'm not leaving because of anyone in particular. However, I admit I do hope to marry eventually and I really want children."

"We all go through this period, you know, especially at your age. But it definitely does get easier to live without a husband and children as you get older. Ask your siblings. Their lives are not always easy."

"I know; I'm not looking for an easier life, just a fuller one. I'm afraid that in the last three years, the religious life has come to seem rather empty to me."

Her voice is funereal as she answers, "Well, then, I guess you have made your choice. I've loved working with you but you're a good teacher now and I'm sure you will find some happiness. I just hope you don't regret your decision when you find that the emptiness of which you speak is part of the human condition. Anyway, good luck." She pats me on the shoulder.

Sister Augusta walks in just then and seeing our serious faces, seems rattled. She's tiptoed around me since she caught Bonnie and me in bed together. "Oh am I interrupting something? I just needed a book."

"No, Sister," I say. "We've finished our chat. Thanks, Sister Bonita; you're a good friend." She grabs my hands with hers for a second. Then I head off to chapel. Sister Bonita's words replay themselves like a broken record. I kneel, struggling to come to terms with them, until the bell rings for Vespers and the other sisters enter. A shaft of late afternoon light paints the ambers and greens of the stained glass across my folded hands.

Chapter XXXVI

Wildfire

By now my plans for leaving are well known among other members of the community. Most of the older sisters treat this information with the utmost discretion, for which I am grateful. They don't discuss it with me, unless I bring it up. I only do that with those closest to me.

However, the infamous Sister Sharon, who is now quite openly involved with Father Redman, is also planning to leave, as is he. She foolishly confides to our principal, Father Mahoney, that not only is she leaving the community but so are Sister Bridget and Sister Faith. Father Mahoney, perhaps in shock or angry vindictiveness because he is losing so many young staff members all at once, tells some students. Like a forest fire in dry timber, word spreads throughout the school. I hadn't planned to tell my students, especially my special drama group, until closer to my time of departure.

One Monday morning, the raging blaze flares up in my face. As I walk away from my first period drama class in the auditorium, a delegation of beloved students surrounds me in a scrum.

"Sister Bridget, Sister Bridget," they yell. "Slow down. We've got to ask you something."

I chuckle with the old joke, "You know I only have one speed. That's fast. If you want to ask me, you'll have to keep up."

Donna names herself spokesperson. She puts her arm around my shoulder and leans close to my ear. "Please say the rumour isn't true – that you're leaving the convent."

I screech to a halt. "Who told you that?"

"Someone heard it from no less than Father Mahoney," Dave, on the other side of me, says. "He said several of the teachers are leaving and you're one of them."

What can I do? I can't lie to these kids, who have made me finally comfortable as a teacher and who have become so special to me. Besides, there is only a month of school left. What harm can it do if I confirm it?

I nod and say in a low voice, "I hadn't wanted you to hear from anyone but me. I would still appreciate it if at least you wouldn't spread this story any further than it's already gone."

Tom interrupts, "Too late, Sister the whole school is talking about it."

My face falls. "Well, even so, please, as friends, don't gossip about it. Yes, I am leaving."

"But why?" asks Candy. "You're just what the Catholic Church needs."

This is not what I want to hear and especially not now, as I am on my way to my second period English class. I need to focus on Shakespeare.

"Listen, folks, I'm really sorry that you found this out as you did but I can't talk about it now; I have to get to class and so do you. Why don't you meet me in the auditorium after school and we'll finish this conversation. Okay?"

"Okay, yeah gotta go. See ya!" They rush off and I compose myself to finish teaching the final act of *Macbeth*. For a moment I picture Macduff holding up the head of Father Mahoney.

After classes, I head to the auditorium. I turn on only a

few of the stage lights, so the main house of the auditorium is quite dark. This way we are unlikely to get intruders. Those of my special group, the ones who'd been drinking beer with me at Mother's Pizza after *The Pied Piper*, the ones who shared a blizzard in Minnesota and a war protest in Madison, turn up to hear more.

Emotion sweeps across the room. Girls are wiping their eyes, and some of the boys bite their lips to hold in their grief. I point out, "You are leaving high school too, so why should it matter so much to you?"

Dave says, "You've given me a whole new view on what a member of the religious life could be like. I actually have been thinking that I might become a priest, since you're so down-to-earth."

I hear echoes of my own reaction to Sister Suzanne's leaving. "Please don't let me change your mind, Dave. You could do anything you want and in the end, you can't base a vocation on what anyone else thinks. It's about you and your relationship to God and your ability to function well as a priest or nun or whatever."

"But you do a great job; nobody better. Why quit? You're my inspiration!"

"Please don't make this more difficult than it is. I've lost faith in my ability to serve God as a nun. I think I'd be better off as a lay woman, for a lot of reasons that I don't want to share."

"Sister Bridget's in love!" Cathy chants.

I turn on her in anger. "I am not but I'm human and I want to be in love. I want to be married. I've changed my mind. It's my life, so please don't tell me not to do it."

This outburst subdues them. "Sorry, Sister, just teasing. I can tell it's been a hard decision," says Cathy.

Donna grabs me and hugs me. "Sister, we're just sad to see you go, because once you leave Eau Claire, we may never see you again. It's not as though we can just drop in at Regis to visit you when we're home on vacation."

"I know. I'll miss you too, but who knows how and where we may meet again. And I promise you I'll never forget you."

"We won't forget you either," Gene says, as he joins in the widening group hug. Then glancing at his watch, "Holy cow, I've got to get to work. Good luck, Sister Bridget. We love you."

"And I love all of you. Now go; we've all got things to do."

That is probably the hardest goodbye.

Chapter XXXVII

Going Home

The final days of school wind down with the usual flurry of big events: honours assembly, baccalaureate, commencement, exams, report cards. I play my role in each of these events as though my life were not undergoing a major change. No graduate should have to suffer because I can't focus enough on my awards presentation speech. I clean the drama area within an inch of its life. I do not want my successor complaining that I'd left things in a mess. I pack my surprisingly large number of books and personal items into my trunk and two suitcases. These routines help to keep me from having any second thoughts that would send me running to Mother Dorothy or writing to the Pope to say, "Whoops! I made a mistake. I'm staying."

No, the die is cast; the game is underway. It is no longer a matter whether I win or lose by my decision but of my walking away from the table altogether.

This I do. What always seemed strange and sad to me is that when nuns leave the convent, there is no big farewell party, or often even any real goodbyes. People leave, then an announcement regarding them is posted. It seems so cold, so devoid of the love we've shared.

So I say my own goodbyes, quietly, individually, some by phone, some in person. Some of us promise to keep in touch. Some make me vow to drop in often. After all, Spring Valley is only an hour's drive away. Realistically, I know that I would be uncomfortable if I were to return even for a visit anytime soon. Besides I am off to graduate school in the fall in Kansas, hundreds of miles south, to finish working on my Master's Degree.

Part of me can hardly suppress the excitement I feel at another new beginning in my life. I am only twenty-six after all. I have a lot of good years left. Naturally I feel very sad to leave my community, the people who have become my second family, people that I love. They have made a lasting impact on my life and leaving them is a physical pain.

~ ~ ~

At last the final day of school arrives. Report cards are handed out and everyone is dismissed in the late morning. My beloved drama students gather around for final hugs and promise to come and visit me at Mom's farm in the summer. I hug some of my colleagues, priests and lay people, as I leave the halls of Regis for perhaps the last time. I avoid the main office where I might run into Father Mahoney, whom I have not forgiven for his error of judgment.

As I re-enter the convent, I stop briefly at the chapel, assuring God that I am not angry with Him. I hope He will forgive me if I am making a terrible mistake. Sister Joan is in the kitchen, fixing lunch. I will skip that, opting instead to eat at my mother's home. Joan has been a friend in need and we hug for a long time. Her eyes water as we break apart but I am fighting the urge to give into tears.

Sister Megan is going to drive me home. She still teaches at nearby Altoona. She has already arrived and is parked at the kitchen entrance. Now I want to go quickly, so she and Joan put my trunk in the back, while I run upstairs, take one last look around my little room – clean as a whistle – and rush downstairs with my two suitcases.

Sister Bonita grabs me in her strong arms and whispers, "I'll pray that you've made the right choice." I swallow and nod, then slip off the ring I received when I professed to be God's bride forever. I bite my lip and hand it to her to return to Mother Dorothy. She slips it into her pocket, then clasps my hands between hers for a moment.

I want no more goodbyes. I can't wait for Megan to turn the key in the ignition. Sister Joan stands in the doorway, waving and weeping.

Normally, Megan and I are never silent on a drive but today our hearts are too full of grief to speak. We turn onto the freeway and I feel freed from nine years of my life. How different that same highway looks with summer unfolding, full of promise. How different from that September day nine years ago. Lilacs bloom, violets wave under trees' outstretched arms, trilliums peek from under thick underbrush. A few broken branches, remnants of winter storms and heavy snow, are scattered along the shoulder.

The winter of my discontent is past. By the time we are halfway home, I give into my grief and euphoria. I weep silently as the miles roll by and the curtains open on the next act of my unfinished play.

Epilogue

My siblings gave me permission to use their real names. Mother's brother Uncle Earl died in 1983; Grandma Rodewald died in 1986; my older brother Jim died in 2002; Mother died in 2004. My dad's sister Bonnie, 88 and brother Jack, 91 are still living in their own homes. The rest of my siblings are alive and well.

As for the rest of the cast of characters, I have changed most of their names to ensure their privacy.

Megan left the convent six years after Bonnie and I did; she taught for many years, retiring in 2004; she remains unmarried. Bonnie married in 1973 and became the mother of two children. She and her husband taught abroad for almost thirty years, mostly in Asia. Faith married and adopted two children. Francesca left the community a few years after I did. I had no contact with her or Monique after I left.

Mother Dorothy died in 2002 after more than a half century as a dedicated nun; Sister Freda, in 2005. Sister Myra died several years before that, as did Sisters Thomas, Jocelyn, Brenda, Adele, Anna, Colleen, Jeanette, Clementine, Augusta, Bonita and others.

Sister Agnes is still living and in her late nineties. Sister Cecelia is in her late eighties. Sister Judy is still a very busy member of the community, as are Sisters Scholastica and Lily.

Father Patrick Gregory is still a practising priest, very involved with catechetical work and retreats. So is Stef, who although his role in the book is minor, he was in fact the celebrant at John's and my wedding. Larry Indigo married his housekeeper and left the priesthood. Barry married another former classmate. Father Will Collie died in 2001. My connection to the other men, Roy, Kyle, Bruce, ended when I left the convent. Except for one picnic at my mother's farm with my favourite drama group in that summer of 1970, I have lost contact with all my students who play roles in this book.

My dream of working abroad came true: I taught in Jamaica from 1972-1975, where I met John. We married in 1974 and moved to Ontario, Canada in 1975. After thirty-four years of teaching English and drama, I retired in 2001. John and I are still happily married. We share a home with Phoenix, our golden retriever.

GLOSSARY

alb – a white vestment reaching to the feet, worn by clergy and servers in the Catholic church

amice – a white linen cloth worn on the neck and shoulders, under the alb, by a priest while celebrating the Eucharist

aspirant – a person having ambitions to follow a particular career, in this case, that of a nun; the name given to younger women who aspire to become members of a religious community

baccalaureate – in American schools, a ceremony, usually with a religious component, to celebrate those people who will be graduating within the week

baptismal name – also known as one's Christian name; the name given to a child at the time of baptism, usually a saint's name, to call upon that saint to protect the child

Benedictine – a monk or nun of a Christian religious order following the rule of St. Benedict, an Italian hermit who established a monastery in the 5th century

biretta – a square cap with three flat projections on top, worn by Roman Catholic clergymen

burse – a flat, square, fabric-covered case in which a folded corporal cloth is carried to and from an altar in church

cape – a sleeveless cloak, often worn by the bishop as his outer garment on special occasions

catechism – a summary of the principles of Christian religion, in the form of questions and answers, for the instruction of Christians

chalice – a large cup or goblet, especially for drinking wine

charge – an assigned task, such as cleaning an area, or acting as the sacristan; a weekly obedience or required duty

chasuble – a sleeveless outer vestment worn by a Catholic priest when celebrating Mass, typically ornate and having a simple hole for the head

cincture – a girdle or belt

community – a group of people living together in one place; the religious family, in this case the Benedictine community of nuns

Compline – a service of evening prayers forming part of the Divine Office of the Western Christian Church

Divine Office – the series of prayers and psalms said or chanted daily by Catholic priests, members of religious orders, and other clergy. Benedictines pray Matins, Lauds, Sext, None, Compline and Vespers, usually at fixed times of the day

Feast of the Immaculate Conception – the Dec. 8th celebration of the doctrine that God preserved the Virgin Mary from the taint of original sin from the moment of her conception

head cantor – the lead singer or chanter in a communal praying of the Divine Office; the one who intones the prayers and others respond

Lauds – a service of morning prayers, part of the Divine Office

Mass – a celebration of the Christian Eucharist or Holy Communion, especially in the Catholic Church; also a musical setting of parts of the liturgy used in the Mass

Matins – the last prayers of the day in the Divine Office

mitre – a tall headdress worn by bishops and senior abbots as a symbol of office, tapering to a point at front and back with a deep cleft between

None – a service of prayers, part of the Divine Office, usually prayed at noon

offertory – one of the essential portions of the Mass, during which the priest offers the bread and wine

postulant – a candidate, especially one seeking admission into a religious order

prie-dieu(x) – a piece of furniture used during prayer, consisting of a kneeling surface and a narrow upright front with a rest for the elbows and books

Prime – part of the Divine Office, said early in the day; no longer in use

priory – a small monastery or nunnery governed by a prior or prioress (superior)

prioress – the head nun in a priory; also called Reverend Mother

rank – position or order in a religious community, based on seniority as well as position, such as an office, including prioress, sub-prioress, etc.

rosary – a form of devotion in which five decades of Hail Marys are repeated, each decade preceded by an Our Father and followed by a Glory Be; a string of beads for keeping count of such a devotion.

sacristan – the person charged with the care of the sacristy and its contents

sacristy – a room in a church where a priest prepares for a service, and where vestments and other things used in services are kept

scapular – a apron-like cover over the nun or monk's habit, easily removed for work

sleevelets – half sleeves, worn by some religious orders to keep the arms from being exposed, since habits tended to have wide sleeves

stole – a priest's silk vestment worn over the shoulders and hanging down to the knees or below

sub-prioress – the nun who is second in command in a community, after the prioress

take the veil – a casual, slangy reference to becoming a nun: receiving the veil as part of a habit in a religious order

Terce – one of the prayers of the Divine Office, originally prayed at three in the morning

tonsure – an act of shaving the top of a monk's or nun's head as a preparation for entering a religious order; also the part of the head left bare by shaving the head

Vespers – the evening prayer, part of the Divine Office, and frequently said along with Compline

vocation – a calling to a state in life

Acknowledgements:

In the autumn of 2000, Ontario schools were under siege from a provincial government slashing funding to education. In the resulting turmoil, Toronto secondary teachers were working to rule – meaning no extra-curricular activities, always my favourite part of education. To lighten the gloomy atmosphere, just before Hallowe'en I challenged my Grade 13 writers' craft class to wear costumes for the holiday. I promised to come as someone from my past.

None of the students took up the challenge, but they were universally shocked when they saw me costumed in a nun's habit. They expected a Rastafarian or a biker chick. A flurry of questions ensued, with them insisting I write my convent story. I'd often had dreams of a temporary return to the religious life, a fantasy more unnerving than frightening. I credit those young people with giving me the impetus I needed to tell my story. When I finished the first draft, I stopped having the dream.

My mother read the first incomplete draft and marvelled at how much she'd learned about her daughter. A childhood friend, Mary Ann Richardson, read it next and begged for more. Thanks to them and to other early readers, whose suggestions I've tried to incorporate as much as possible. These include Sister Lucille Hubmann, Fred and Georgie Kennedy, Peggy Arges, Sandra Jin, Mary Ellen McQuay, Myrna Marcelline, Betty Nelson, Julie Chang, Jeanne Adler and Christine Stevenson.

Thanks also to the Writers' Circle of Durham Region which encouraged me to believe in myself as a writer, especially the Writing Fairy Dorothea Helms. Editor Rachelle Lerner read the first fifty pages and through her suggestions, made me realize I had a long path to travel to make this a book. Ruth Walker's humorous and encouraging edits of two drafts of the manuscript were invaluable, helping me to open up more ("Come on, Karen, DISH!"). I'm grateful also to the members of my small writing circle WIP (Works in Progress) – Kevin Craig, Barbara Hunt, Sherry Hinman, Myrna Marcelline, Heather O'Connor, Marea Rockburn, Heather Tucker, Susan Statham and Collette Yvonne – for helping me hone my writing skills. Special thanks also to Collette and to Francine Pelletier, journalist and filmmaker, for endorsing the book.

My former English teacher Dr. Kenneth Ames, Jr., encouraged my writing from the beginning of my high school career. He also inspired me for a lifetime with the motto, "Be happy in your work." I'm so grateful for that good advice.

Thanks to Richard M. Grove (Tai) of Hidden Brook Press for the final substantive editing, pushing me to lift the veil even more on a life so unfamiliar to the average person. Richard also is the one-man band whose efforts and guidance finally resulted in a book. Paul Prechner copyedited the book and made several valuable observations of issues I'd overlooked. I appreciate his work.

I'm grateful to my family for their interest and encouragement in the project. Thanks also to the sisters of St. Benedict for their kindness and support through nine years of sharing their lives and for still treating me like one of the family whenever I visit. Special thanks to Sister Judy Kramer for enriching some stories, and to Jeanne Adler who jogged my memory to recall events of forty years ago.

Finally, my endless gratitude to John whose encouragement, technical computer skills, constant support and love helped make this dream a reality.

Credits:

Lines from "Both Sides Now" reprinted with permission from Alfred Publishing Co. Inc. Words and music by Joni Mitchell copyright 1967.

Biographical Sketch of Author:

After leaving the convent in 1970, Karen L. Cole earned an MA from the University of Kansas and taught for a year in Missouri.

In 1972, she embarked on a teaching adventure in Savanna-La-Mar, Jamaica. It was there that she met her husband, John, a Canadian of English background. In 1974 they married and in 1975, they returned to Ontario where they both taught in Scarborough schools for nearly thirty years. When not working, the couple gardened avidly and travelled the world extensively.

After retirement in 2001, Karen settled down to becoming a more serious writer. Her articles have appeared in The Word Weaver, a publication of the Writers Circle of Durham Region and in the Metroland papers.

In 2008, her story "Quilts and Quirks" appeared in an anthology on grandmothers, *Wisdom of Old Souls* published by Hidden Brook Press. She has written an unpublished novel about Jamaica, *Southern Exposure* and is working on another, *Letters to Louise*. *Lifting the Veil* is Karen's first full-length work.

www.ingramcontent.com/pod-product-compliance
Lightning Source LLC
Chambersburg PA
CBHW021055080526
44587CB00010B/256